THE
UNDER
$15.00
GOOD
EATING GUIDE

Daniel Young

Ra Re/Peanut Butter Book

WYNWOOD™ Press
New York, New York

Library of Congress Cataloging-in-Publication Data

Young, Daniel.
  The under $15 good eating guide: New York's 100 best
inexpensive dining adventures / Daniel Young.

       p.   cm.
    Includes indexes.
    ISBN 0-922066-00-0: $9.95
1. Restaurants, lunch rooms, etc.—New York (N.Y.)—Guide-books.
2. New York (N.Y.)—Description—1981—Guide-books.   I. Title.
II.   Title: Under fifteen dollar good eating guide.
TX907.3.N72N49   1989
647′.96747′—dc19   89-5255
                                                            CIP

Copyright © 1989 by Daniel Young
Published by WYNWOOD™ Press
New York, New York
Printed in the United States of America

For my parents

Route	Operates Between	Times	Manhattan	Bronx	Brooklyn
1 Broadway-7 Av Local	242 Street, Bronx and South Ferry, Manhattan	All Times	Local	Local	
1 Broadway-7 Av Local	137 Street, and South Ferry, Manhattan	Weekdays, 8:15 AM-4:45 PM	Local		
2 7 Avenue Express	241 Street, Bronx and Flatbush Avenue, Brooklyn	All Times	Express, 96 St-Chambers St	All Stops	All Stops
3 7 Avenue Express	148 Street, Manhattan and New Lots Avenue, Brooklyn	All Times, except Nights and early Sunday AM	Express, 96 St-Chambers St		All Stops
3 Shuttle	148 Street and 135 Street, Manhattan	Nights and early Sunday AM	All Stops; connects with No. 2 at 135 St		
4 Lexington Av Express	Woodlawn, Bronx and Utica Avenue, Brooklyn	All Times	Express, 125 St-Brooklyn Bridge; Local, 1 AM-5 AM	All Stops; skips 138 St, to Manhattan AM, from Manhattan PM	Express, Boro Hall-Utica Av
4 Lexington Av Express	Woodlawn, Bronx and New Lots Avenue, Brooklyn	Nights and Early Sunday AM	Express, 125 St-Brooklyn Bridge; Local, 1 AM-5 AM	All Stops	All Stops; skips Hoyt St
5 Lexington Av Express	Dyre Avenue, Bronx and Bowling Green, Manhattan	All Times, except 12 Mid-5 AM	Express, 125 St-Brooklyn Bridge	All Stops	
5 Lexington Av Express	Dyre Avenue, Bronx and Flatbush Av, Brooklyn	Rush Hours	Express, 125 St-Brooklyn Bridge	Express, E 180 St-149 St-3 Av, to Manhattan AM, from Manhattan PM	Express, Boro Hall-Franklin Av
5 Shuttle	Dyre Avenue and E 180 Street, Bronx	Late Nights (12 Mid-5 AM)		All Stops; connects with No. 2 at E 180 St	
5 Lexington Av Exp-Bronx Thru Express	241 Street, Bronx and Flatbush Avenue, Brooklyn	Rush Hours	Express, 125 St-Brooklyn Bridge	Express, E 180 St-149 St-3 Av, to Manhattan AM, from Manhattan PM	Express, Boro Hall-Franklin Av

Line	Route	Times	Service	Service
6 Lexington Av Local	Pelham Bay Park, Bronx and Brooklyn Bridge, Manhattan	All Times, except 1 AM–5 AM	Local	Local
6 Lexington Av Local	East 177 Street, Bronx and Brooklyn Bridge, Manhattan	Weekdays, 6:30 AM–8 PM	Local	Local
6 Lexington Av Local-Pelham Express	Pelham Bay Park, Bronx and Brooklyn Bridge, Manhattan	Weekdays, 6:30 AM–8 PM	Local	Express, E 177 St– 3 Av–138 St, to Manhattan AM, from Manhattan PM
6 Shuttle	Pelham Bay Park, Bronx and 125 Street, Manhattan	Late Nights (1 AM–5AM)	Local; connects with No. 4 at 125 St.	Local
7 Flushing Local	Main Street, Flushing and Times Square, Manhattan	All Times	Local	Queens Local
S 42nd Street Shuttle	Times Square and Grand Central, Manhattan	All Times		
S Franklin Av Shuttle	Franklin Avenue and Prospect Park, Brooklyn	All Times		
+ JFK Express	57 St–6 Av, Manhattan and Howard Beach-JFK Airport, Queens	From 57 St, 5AM–12 Midnight, from JFK 6AM–1AM; every 20-24 minutes. Extra fare collected on train. Connects at JFK station with bus to all terminals.	Note: Carries local passengers between 57 St–6 Av and 47-50 St weekday evenings 9PM–AM. No premium fare charged between these 2 stations.	

SUBWAY SERVICE GUIDE

Route	Operates Between	Times	Manhattan	Queens	Brooklyn	Bronx
Ⓐ 8 Av Express	207 St, Manhattan and Lefferts Blvd, Queens.	All times	Express, 168 St-Canal St; Midnight hrs: Local	Local	Express Hoyt-Schermerhorn Sts-Euclid Av (see C) rush and midday; local all other times.	
Ⓐ 8 Av Express	207 St, Manhattan and Far Rockaway, Queens	All times, except midnight hours (see H)	Express, 168 St-Canal St	Local	Av (see C) rush and midday; local all other times.	
Ⓒ 8 Av Local	Bedford Park Blvd, Bronx or 145 St, Manhattan and Euclid Av, Brooklyn or Rockaway Park, Queens	Weekdays, 6AM-9PM	Local; from 145 St midday	Local	Local	Local from Bedford Park rush hours
Ⓒ 8 Av Local	145 St, Manhattan and World Trade Center, Manhattan	Evenings and weekends	Local			
Ⓔ 8 Av Local	Jamaica Center (Parsons / Archer) and World Trade Center, Manhattan	All times	Local	Express, Union Tpke-Queens Plaza		
Ⓗ Rockaway Shuttle	Euclid Av, Brooklyn or Broad Channel, Queens and Rockaway Park, Queens	Evenings to Euclid Av; Weekends to Broad Channel (see C other times)		Local; connects with A at Broad Channel (weekends)	Local; connects with A at Euclid Av (evenings)	
Ⓗ Rockaway Shuttle	Euclid Av, Brooklyn to Rockaway Park to Far Rockaway and back to Euclid Av	Midnight hours		Local	Local; connects with A at Euclid Av	
Ⓙ Nassau Street Local	Jamaica Center (Parsons / Archer), Queens and Broad Sts., Manhattan	All times	Local (skips Bowery 6am-8pm weekdays)	Local except rush hours; rush hours, skip-stop express 121 St-Myrtle Av to Manhattan AM, from Manhattan PM (see Z)	Express, Myrtle Av-Marcy Av, to Manhattan AM, from Manhattan PM (see M)	
Ⓜ Nassau Street Local	Metropolitan Av, Queens and 9 Av, Brooklyn	Weekdays, 6 AM-8 PM	Local	Local	Express, Pacific St-36 St	
Ⓜ Nassau Street Local	Metropolitan Av, Queens and Bay Parkway, Brooklyn	Rush hours from Bay Parkway AM, to Bay Parkway PM	Local	Local	Express, Pacific St-36 St	
Ⓜ Shuttle	Metropolitan Av, Queens and Myrtle Av, Brooklyn	Evenings, Nights and Weekends		Local	Local; connects with J at Myrtle Av	
Ⓝ Nassau Street Local	Jamaica Center (Parsons/Archer), Queens and Broad St., Manhattan	Rush hours from Parsons-Jamaica AM, from Broad St PM	Local (skips Bowery)	Skip-stop express 121 St-Myrtle Av (see J)	Express, Myrtle Av-Marcy Av.	

SUBWAY SERVICE GUIDE

			Monday through Friday rush hours, middays and evenings	Express 7 Av-W 4 St		Express Pacific St-36 St, skips DeKalb Av rush hours and midday
Ⓑ	Av of Americas (6 Av) Express	168 St, Manhattan and Coney Island, Brooklyn				Express Pacific St-36 St, skips DeKalb Av rush hours and midday
Ⓑ	Av of Americas (6 Av) Express	57 St-6 Av, Manhattan and Coney Island, Brooklyn	Weekends	Express 57 St-W 4 St		Express Pacific St-36 St
Ⓑ	Shuttle	36 St and Coney Island, Brooklyn	Midnight hours			Local; connects with N and R at 36 St
Ⓓ	Av of Americas (6 Av) Express	205 St, Bronx and Coney Island, Brooklyn	All times	Express 145 St-W 4 St		Local, except rush hours: Express Fordham Rd-145 St, to Manhattan AM, from Manhattan PM (see C)
Ⓕ	Av of Americas (6 Av) Local	179 St, Jamaica and Coney Island, Brooklyn	All times except midnight hours	Local	All times, Express 71 Av-Queens Plaza; Weekdays, Express 179 St-Queens Plaza	Local
Ⓕ	Av of Americas (6 Av) Local	179 St, Jamaica and Kings Highway, Brooklyn	Rush hours	Local		Local
Ⓕ	Av of Americas (6 Av) Local	57 St-6 Av, Manhattan and Coney Island, Brooklyn	Midnight hours	Local		Local
Ⓖ	Av of Americas (6 Av) Express	57 St-6 Av, Manhattan and Brighton Beach, Brooklyn	Weekdays 6AM-9PM	Express 57 St-W 4 St		Express DeKalb Av-Brighton Beach
Ⓖ	Brooklyn-Queens Crosstown	71-Continental Avs, Forest Hills and Smith-9 Sts, Brooklyn	Weekdays, 6AM-9PM		Local	Local
Ⓖ	Brooklyn-Queens Crosstown	Queens Plaza, Queens and Smith-9 Sts, Brooklyn	Evenings, Nights and Weekends		Local; connects with R at Queens Plaza	Local
Ⓛ	14 St-Canarsie Local	8 Av, Manhattan and Rockaway Parkway, Brooklyn	All times	Local		Local
N	Broadway Local	Ditmars Blvd, Astoria and Coney Island, Brooklyn	All times	Local		Evenings and Weekends, Express Pacific St-59 St
R	Broadway Local	179 St, Jamaica and 95 St, Brooklyn	All times	Local		Local

Acknowledgments

The dream of sharing with you my passion for discovering and rediscovering New York's best bargain bites was realized only with the encouragement and undying enthusiasm of six extraordinary people: Steve Yahn, Andrea Rock, Arthur Schwartz, Steve Biondolillo, Roy Young, and William Young. I owe each a lifetime of great pizzas.

I also want to express my gratitude to the good friends (and courageous dining companions) who joined me on the quest and made each night out a memorable one: Alan Cohen, Julia Martin, June Rogoznica, Steven Forbis, Leslie Laurence, Fran Collin, Kevin Ray, Rich Schreiber, Alan Reiter, Jennifer Schecter, Linda Williams, and Marco Moreira.

And special thanks to Mark Giles, my Brooklyn guru, for his help with the manuscript and the many laughs over numerous lunches and dinners.

D.Y.

Contents

Introduction

Among New York's seven million food critics, my late grandfather was perhaps the most concise. A baker by trade, he had the same review for all of his favorite eateries. "First class!" he'd say after the telling first bite. "There's no better." It didn't matter that the places in question served nothing more deluxe than a frank and French fries. To him they were all first class.

He understood the wonderful paradox about dining out in New York: Many of the city's most highly valued restaurants are also among the lowest priced. In fact, only those willing to drop pretensions instead of cash discover all the remarkable flavors in the world's most diverse melting pot.

My hungry hunt for the city's best inexpensive dining adventures started out as a single-minded search for the perfect pierogi, the consummate conchiglie, the existential egg cream. The fruits of these days and nights of dining dangerously, however, were much sweeter. This guide, aside from being about good eating, is also a compilation of ways to enjoy the multiplicity of this city with people you care about. If it helps you find the settings for shared friendships, good times, and an enhanced taste for everything New York, then it will have been a success.

Nevertheless, the highlight and lowlight of my dining experiences had little to do with food, price, ambiance, or friendship. I was eating alone at a West Village restaurant and couldn't help noticing that three gorgeous gals seated across the room were staring at me incessantly. I'm no Cary Grant, but I'm no Elephant Man either, so I was quite surprised and excited. As I got up to introduce myself to my admirers, I glanced behind me and noticed the specials menu for the first time. Humiliated, I returned to an unsympathetic plate of eggplant lasagna.

That was an important lesson for a restaurant critic: Always ask about the specials.

Notes on Using This Guide

In choosing the top one hundred restaurants from among the three hundred-plus I've reviewed for the New York *Daily News* during the past three and a half years, ethnic and neighborhood diversity were important considerations. This guide describes restaurants of twenty-nine different nationalities in thirty-five different neighborhoods.

The ultimate criterion, however, was much more personal. About each restaurant I asked myself, "Would I want to take a close friend there?" If the answer was yes, it's in the guide.

"Under $15" means that one person can eat a complete and satisfying meal for less than $15. This allows up to $8.50 for entrees (the average price is listed above each description) and the remainder to cover the cost of an appetizer, dessert, or beverage.

Restaurants are divided into five classifications: Ethnic Treasure 🏛 , A Little Romance ❤ , Funky Casual 👟 , Wholesome Hideaway 🦪 , and Positively NYC 🍎 . Though I consider most to be Ethnic Treasures, places conducive to dating (A Little Romance), pop-fashion dining (Funky Casual), healthy eating (Wholesome Hideaway), or New York–style munching (Positively NYC) are thus distinguished.

I visited all eateries accepted (and rejected) for this guide anonymously and paid for my own meals. "Pièce de résistance" (outstanding item) selections were all personal judgments.

Most restaurants that do not serve alcohol will

allow you to bring your own. Credit cards, when accepted, have been abbreviated as follows: AE, American Express; DC, Diners Club; MC, MasterCard; V, Visa. Telephone numbers are in the 212 area code, unless a 718 is indicated for Brooklyn, Queens, and Staten Island locations.

Although specific information about the restaurants was updated immediately prior to publication, some details—prices, hours, menu selections, etc.—may be as perishable as a pound of porgy. Even subway routes are altered to accommodate track work and bridge repairs. It never hurts to call first.

Daniel Young

THE

UNDER

$15.⁰⁰

GOOD
EATING GUIDE

Afghanistan Kebab House

764 Ninth Ave., near West 51st St.
Clinton, Manhattan
307-1612
Open: Mon.–Sat. 12:30 P.M.–10 P.M.
By subway: C, E to 50th St.
Average price per entree: $8
Alcohol: none
Credit: none
Reservations: none
Classification: Ethnic Treasure
Pièce de résistance: lamb tikka kebab

If you like the charcoal flavor of chicken, burgers, and shish kebabs cooked on the backyard
barbecue, chances are you'll flip for the meats
broiled over wood charcoal at the Afghanistan
Kebab House. Chunks of well-marinated lamb,
chicken, beef, or vegetables are charred to perfection in a tandoor oven and served with basmati rice
and lettuce and tomato topped with yogurt dressing. Two personal favorites are lamb tikka kebab
(with reasonably tender chunks of lamb from the
thigh portion) and half-chicken tandoori. All selections are well-spiced but not hot.

Afghanistan Kebab House is a small, modest
shop brightened only slightly by its folkloric deco-
rations: colorful dresses and vests hung along the
walls; throw rugs, covered by clear plastic, over
each table. Sorry, only the kebabs are for sale.

Arturo's

106 West Houston St., at Thompson St.
Greenwich Village, Manhattan
677-3820
Open: Mon. & Tues. 4 P.M.–midnight, Wed. & Thurs.
  till 1 A.M., Fri. & Sat. till 2 A.M., Sun. 3 P.M.–midnight
By subway: 6 to Bleecker St.; A, C, E to West 4th St.; F
  to Broadway/Lafayette
Average price per pizza: $12
Alcohol: yes
Credit: AE, MC, V
Reservations: none
Classification: A Little Romance
Pièce de résistance: Fiesta pizza

Arturo's is not an elegant establishment, but the corner by the border of SoHo and the Village is a favorite locale for cheap dates. The cool breeze of live, light jazz blows the steam off sizzling, coal-oven-baked pies noted for their crisp crust, sweet 'n' zesty tomato-sauce topping, and matchmaking capabilities. Dates who discard crust ends like fish bones tend to be neurotic, but get along nicely with the shameless scavengers who scoop them up.

The available pizza toppings are anchovies, bacon, eggplant, meatballs, mushroom, pepperoni, peppers and onions, sausage, and in combination, Arturo's Fiesta: sausage, mushroom, peppers, and onions. Arturo's also offers a full menu of Italian food, but most nonpasta entrees, though reasonably priced, are a little out of this guide's price range. Still, the mixed antipasto makes a fine pizza prelude.

Choice tables closer to the bar and the music are

worth a short wait, though I don't mind sitting next to the photo of Lou Costello that's hanging in the side dining room. If a date happens to be going well, I like to give Lou a knowing wink and plan a stroll over to Caffe Dante (79 MacDougal Street, near Bleecker Street) for dessert.

Aunt Flo's

79 Warren St., near West Broadway
Financial District, Manhattan
608-6155
Open: Mon.–Fri. 7 A.M.–9 P.M., Sat. 3 P.M.–10 P.M.
By subway: 1, 2, 3, A, C, E to Chambers St.
Average price per lunch: $5.50
Alcohol: beer and wine
Credit: none
Reservations: none
Classification: Ethnic Treasure
Pièce de résistance: barbecued ribs

Sorry to disillusion those of you already loyal to Aunt Flo's, but the restaurant's food is neither prepared, served, nor conceived by a loving woman named Flo. This cafeteria-style soul food place is run by three guys from Queens, coworkers at the phone company who've obviously made a great connection. Each weekday Aunt Flo's cooks up three squares of first-rate soul food for people working in and around the World Trade Center. And now they're open Saturdays too.

Although the restaurant looks like any generic, fast-food place, most everything tastes as though it were cooked in somebody's mother's (or aunt's) house. The four lunches, priced $4 to $7 and available daily, are succulent barbecued ribs, juicy southern-fried chicken, crispy fried pork chops, and West Indian-style curried chicken or beef. In addition, there's a different special each day: short ribs, oxtail stew, fried fish, turkey wings, etc. All lunches and dinners come with two sides, including fresh collard greens and fresh candied yams. Nothing is canned.

They've also got a decent $3 breakfast special of two eggs, grits or home fries, toast, coffee, and bacon (slab or regular), sausage (regular, sage, or hot), or ham. Dinner prices are $2 higher than at lunch. Don't leave without tasting the sweet-potato pie.

Aunt Suzie

247 Fifth Ave., near Carroll St.
Park Slope, Brooklyn
(718) 788-3377
Open: Sun.–Thurs. 5:30 P.M.–10 P.M., Fri. & Sat. till 11:30 P.M.
By subway: N, R to Union St.
Average price per entree: $7.50
Alcohol: beer and wine
Credit: none
Reservations: none
Classification: Ethnic Treasure
Pièce de résistance: chicken sorrentino

The two antique gas stoves displayed in the storefront of this Italian restaurant send a heart-warming message to lost Brooklyn souls. The eatery may owe its handsome look and very exist-ence to the new and expanding prosperity of the Park Slope neighborhood, but the cooking descends from the original Aunt Suzie's of Benson-hurst and its immigrant family traditions. "Yuppies don't cook," says owner Irene LoRe, explaining her move to the Slope. "If you want to open a restaurant, you go where the yuppies are."

What's most distinctive about the new locale is the assortment of old oak dining tables that fill the spacious restaurant. This may be the only antiques gallery in the world where they let you eat baked rigatoni. During my first visit, I felt lost without the obligatory checkered tablecloths, all the time envisioning the disastrous consequences of my spilling tomato sauce on something priceless.

For starters, the hot antipasto ($5.90) is first rate and more than enough for two to share. If you're like me, you'll sop up every last trace of the garlicky sauce and breadcrumbs with their addictive, seeded Italian bread. (If you share hot antipasto with me, here's the deal: You get the extra baked clam; I get to clean off the plate.)

Pastas are $3.90 to $5.90; entrees start at $5.90 (only seafood dishes jump over $10) and come with a good-sized bowl of pasta marinara or salad (no contest: take the pasta). Give serious consideration to the chicken sorrentino—thin, delicate cutlets with eggplant, mozzarella, and diced prosciutto. Also recommended: shrimp verde (with broccoli and mushrooms) and the juicy, tender, flavorful double pork chop with peppers and mushrooms.

For dessert, the Italian cheesecake, fresh from Campania Pastry Shop in Bensonhurst, is a light-heavyweight champ. Ahhh, if you knew Aunt Suzie! . . .

Barba Yiorgis O Ksenihtis

31–84 33rd St., near Broadway
Astoria, Queens
(718) 956-6096
Open: seven days 24 hours
By subway: N to Broadway
Average price per entree: $5.50
Alcohol: beer and wine
Credit: none
Reservations: none
Classification: Ethnic Treasure
Pièce de résistance: taramosalata

Lunchtime comes at noon, 6 P.M., midnight, even 3 A.M. at Barba Yiorgis O Ksenihtis (in English, Uncle George the Night Owl). The Greek restaurant stays open all night for the working men (and women, though they are a distinct minority) of Astoria—cabbies, restaurant workers, etc.—for whom 9-to-5 means only the short odds on a racehorse. Still, anyone can stop in anytime for good, home cooking at remarkably low prices.

Though Spartan in decor and origin, Barba Yiorgis is a nice-looking shop with checkered tablecloths, wood-framed maps of the Greek isles along the walls, and a white tin ceiling. Since there are no menus and some waiters do not speak English, ordering can be difficult for non-Greeks. During my first visit I peeked into the kitchen and ordered by pointing.

Barba Yiorgis is known for his taramosalata, the potted fish-roe appetizer, which is difficult to prepare and not always available (I'd love to spread it on a bagel; call me irresponsible). He also does a splendid job with charcoal-grilled fish, mostly flavored with olive oil and garnished with watercress and parsley; the char-grilled skate fish (*salaki* in Greek) is sweet and delicious and $6. For that price or less, you can also enjoy such daily specials as fried squid, rice meatballs in soup, or lamb with potatoes, beans, or pasta—all hearty Greek food for a neighborhood that never sleeps. Great desserts are less than a block away at Omonia Cafe (*see* page 97).

Benny's New York

359 East 68th St., at First Ave.
Upper East Side, Manhattan
249-5460
Open: Mon.–Sat. 11 A.M.–11 P.M.
By subway: 6 to 68th St.
Average price per combo plate: lunch, $4.95; dinner, $5.95
Alcohol: none
Credit: none
Reservations: none
Classification: Wholesome Hideaway
Pièce de résistance: lemon chicken

Moviegoers, shoppers, or anyone on a tight schedule (that covers about 99 percent of New York's population) should look to Benny's contemporary Middle Eastern cafe for quick, quality eats. Say it's 6:50 P.M. and you want to catch the 7:35 P.M. show at the Beekman. Then there's still time for a plate of ginger chicken, crisp broccoli salad, and sesame soy noodles with mixed vegetables at Benny's. And all that good food actually costs less than the movie.

The menu consists of seventeen such Middle

Eastern or Oriental-influenced entrees served at room temperature. A combo plate with a choice of any three is $4.95 for weekday matinees, $5.95 weekdays after 4 P.M. and all day Saturday. These trios are a swell idea since you'll want to sample as much of Benny's fresh, wholesome, expertly seasoned cooking as you can. Particularly tasteworthy: luscious lemon chicken (perfect chunks of chicken breast marinated in lemon, basil, and mint), vegetable lasagna (three cheeses and unusually firm and flavorful veggies), Benny's maza (hummus, tabbouleh, and pita bread), and eggplant sauté (chopped eggplant sauteed in tomatoes, garlic, coriander, and roasted peppers). All choices are openly displayed in a window case that's replenished with fresh food throughout the day.

Benny's also serves nice cakes, cappuccino, and espresso for dessert—if you don't need to rush off and catch a movie.

Bernstein-On-Essex St.

135 Essex St., near Rivington St.
Lower East Side, Manhattan
473-3900
Open: Sun.–Thurs. 8 A.M.–1 A.M., Fri. 8 A.M.–3 P.M.
By subway: F to Delancey St.; J, M to Essex St.
Average price per sandwich: $6
Alcohol: beer and wine
Credit: AE, DC, MC, V
Reservations: not necessary
Classification: Ethnic Treasure
Pièce de résistance: corned beef sandwich

A great kosher delicatessen is hard to find in New York, which means its hard to find, period. I bounced despairingly from deli to deli, looking for a nice kosher corned beef to recommend for this guide, before I crossed Delancey Street and found one still worth getting excited about. Bernstein-On-Essex, a.k.a. Schmulka Bernstein, helped me appreciate the breadth of those early disappointments.

As a result, I've devised a new, more sophisticated method for comparing corned beef and pastrami sandwiches. I keep a record of the length of time and number of chews it takes to finish them. One with dry, tough, stringy, chewy meat, for example, might last twenty-two minutes or 600 chews. Another with moist, tasty, tender meat that instantly surrenders to the teeth would probably disappear in close to five minutes or 125 chews. Bernstein's sufficiently fatty corned beef and soft, hot pastrami were received for four minutes, the *Under $15 Good Eating Guide's* highest rating; tongue (naturally not as tender) got a most respectable eight.

Those ratings do not include time taken out for the fabulous, crunchy cole slaw, the decent deli fries, a Dr. Brown's Cel-Ray tonic, or the dreamy apple strudel, with its impossibly light, flaky pastry shell. Oy-oy-oy!

Bernstein-On-Essex is also well-known for introducing glatt kosher Chinese food to New York. The entrees on that part of the menu, however, are too expensive to qualify for this guide. Chinese waiters and some decorative touches are employed to give the place a Beijing-On-Essex feel—the rear dining room/banquet hall succeeds at appearing dignified—but the overall impression remains of an informal, Lower East Side delicatessen.

Broadway Diner

590 Lexington Ave., at East 52nd St.
Midtown East, Manhattan
486-8838
Open: Mon.–Fri. 7 A.M.–10 P.M., Sat. 8 A.M.–10 P.M.
By subway: 6 to 51st St.; E, F to Lexington Ave.

1726 Broadway, at West 55th St.
Midtown West, Manhattan
765-0909
Open: Sun.–Thurs. 7 A.M.–11 P.M., Fri. & Sat. 8 A.M.–
midnight
By subway: N, Q, R to 57th St.; 1, A, C, D to 59th
St./Columbus Circle

Average price per lunch: $7
Alcohol: yes
Credit: none
Reservations: none
Classification: Funky Casual
Pièce de résistance: chicken breast sandwich with avo-
cado mayo

These two upscale, midtown descendents of the
classic Art Deco diner are perfect pit stops for
funky-casual lunches and pretheater, prewhatever
munchies. The Broadway location is convenient to
Carnegie Hall, City Center, the Biograph Cinema,
several Broadway theaters, and two penny arcades.
Prices are higher than other coffee shops, but not
unreasonable considering the sharp decor and sur-
prisingly good food. Both are acceptable places to
bring a date.

What might be unsettling to some is the cheerful

lunchtime clatter—there's nothing to absorb sound at the Lexington Avenue Broadway Diner except people and mashed potatoes. But oh boy, what a fun menu! Side orders like shoestring French fries and mango salsa. Condiments like avocado- or horseradish-flavored mayonnaise. There's no soup du jour but a "Different Soup Every Day." I told the waitress I'd like to order a "Different Soup Every Day." She said, "That's fine, but whadda ya want today?" A house specialty, confit of warm duck salad, is not exactly a truck driver's favorite.

The mountainous salads ($5.95 to $7.95) are superb if you've got about two hours (and two bodies) for lunch; otherwise try one of the grilled sandwiches like eggplant with onions, mozzarella and basil, or chicken breast with avocado mayo (order extra avo-mayo on the side). Eight-ounce burgers on kaiser rolls are first rate. And the desserts? Oooh . . . that hot apple pie à la mode is what classic diners are about.

By the way, tater fans, on which side of the mashed-potato controversy are you? Some feel mashed potatoes prepared lumpy, as they are at the Broadway Diner, are authentic, the way Mom would make 'em. Others like 'em smooth, insisting that most moms just don't know how to make mashed potatoes right.

Budnamujip

41–17 Union St., at Barclay Ave.
Flushing, Queens
(718) 461-0363
Open: seven days 11:00 A.M.–1 A.M.
By subway: 7 to Main St.
Average price per entree: $7.50
Alcohol: beer and saki
Credit: AE
Reservations: not necessary
Classification: Ethnic Treasure
Pièce de résistance: dan jang jigae

Union Street may be just a few Darryl Strawberry home runs away from Shea Stadium, but the favorite pastime in the Seoul of Flushing has more to do with chopsticks than baseball bats. The country Korean cooking at Budnamujip plays to near-capacity crowds throughout its 365-day schedule. And small wonder. The place is friendly and cozy, all but two of the entrees are priced from $5.95 to $8.95, and the quality of the food, at least to this novice Bud-taster, is major league.

The specialty of the house, according to one waitress, is a dish that does not appear on the English menu, sam kay tang. This turns out to be nothing more exotic than a splendid rendition of chicken in the pot, stuffed with sticky rice, garlic, and ginseng. Mothers-in-law traditionally serve this dish to their sons-in-law to give them stamina and good health. (Now this is a tradition I can get behind.) Another recommended dish is dan jang jigae, a soothing soup with bean curd, zucchini, scallions, a little green pepper, and a few pea-sized baby clams. Although the beef dish bulgoki is not barbecued at the table, as is often the custom at Korean restaurants, and the meat itself is less than prime, the oniony, sesame-based marinade makes it worth ordering. The go choo pajun–rice pancakes with chives and small pieces of octopus served with a soy and sesame dip–may be a little too greasy, but it will always be a big hit at my table.

For appetizers, gratis servings of delicious kimchee (cabbage pickled in salt and hot chili pepper), along with pickled radishes, bean sprouts, and sliced cucumber, arrive before you actually order and are replenished throughout the meal.

Cabana Carioca

123 West 45th St., near Sixth Ave.
Theater District, Manhattan
581-8088
Open: Sun.–Thurs. noon–11 P.M., Fri. & Sat. till midnight.
By subway: 1, 2, 3, B, D, F, N, Q, R to 42nd St.
Price per buffet lunch: $4.95 or $8.95
Alcohol: yes
Credit: AE, DC, MC, V (cash only for lunch buffet)
Reservations: none
Classification: Ethnic Treasure
Pièce de résistance: lunch buffet

Only a dunce would describe Cabana Carioca's dinner menu as being too expensive. That happens to be my unfortunate task, since the price for dinner at this Brazilian restaurant, though an exceptional value by any measure, is a little too high for the $15 barrier. Fortunately I can redeem myself by telling you about their two incredible lunch buffets, real "Rio Grandes."

The food at the two all-you-can-eat buffets is identical; only the price, atmosphere, and hours are different. The $8.95 buffet on the dressier first floor is open seven days, noon to 3 P.M. The $4.95 buffet on the drabber third floor is open during those same hours on weekdays only.

The lavish lunch buffet is made up of three stations: cold, hot, and dessert. On any given day the cold station might include chick-peas, kidney beans, medium shrimp, squid, tuna salad, potato salad (more like a vegetable mayonnaise), and lettuce and tomato salad. Atop the steam table might be found fried fish, garlicky broiled chicken, veal stew, roast pork, rice, fried potato discs, chopped collard greens, and the house specialty, feijoada, a peasant's hodgepodge of different meats—Portuguese sausage, pigs knuckles, beef, whatever's available—in black beans. Try topping the feijoada with mandioca flour and hot red pepper sauce and you may find yourself going back for seconds and thirds. Dessert choices include supersweet shredded cocount, canned fruit cocktail, flan, and soft-serve ice cream.

Cafe Edison

228 West 47th St., near Seventh Ave.
Theater District, Manhattan
354-0368
Open: Mon.–Sat. 6:15 A.M.–10 P.M., Sun. till 3 P.M.
By subway: 1 to 50th St.; N, R to 49th St.
Average price per lunch special: $7.50
Alcohol: none
Credit: none
Reservations: none
Classification: Positively NYC
Pièce de résistance: kasha varnishkes

One Monday I was sitting in the Polish Tea Room in the Cafe Edison in the Edison Hotel. I was minding my own business, which on this particular day happened to be matzo ball soup, pot roast, rice pudding, and coffee, when I spotted Neil Simon in the VIP Room, looking a little weary. Maybe he'd been up all night doctoring a new play. "You think he'd feel better if I sent him over a plate of kasha varnishkes?" I said to my friend. "It's the stuff that Tonys are made of." But I left the Jewish mothering to Frances, who pampers Broadway big shots with her Jewish/Eastern European–style cooking. Hey Mr. Producer, how about some blintzes?

Theater people love to shmooze at Cafe Edison. They seem to feel at home in its grotesque interior, which looks like a routine coffee shop dropped into an ornate dining room whose elegance is long past. They obviously come for the food: pot roast, brisket, veal goulash, boiled beef in the pot, chopped liver—everything their grandmas used to make. Lunch specials, which include two sides, a choice of eight soups, and a beverage, usually run about $7 or $8. And, oh my, those kasha varnishkes—oniony, well-oiled buckwheat groats with bowtie noodles. Wow! Soup and kasha is not a bad $3 meal. For breakfast, there's decent challah French toast and banana-walnut pancakes, though tables are filled primarily by hotel guests.

And you don't have to worry about Neil. Frances fixed him up with a bowl of cabbage soup.

Caribe

117 Perry St., at Greenwich St.
Greenwich Village, New York
255-9191
Open: Sun.–Thurs. 5 P.M.–11 P.M., Fri. & Sat. till midnight
By subway: 1 to Christopher St.
Average price per entree: $8
Alcohol: Yes
Credit: none
Reservations: none
Classification: Funky Casual
Pièce de résistance: chicken Caribe

Don't get me wrong, Caribe is a terrific restaurant. It's just that they put so many potted palms inside, the place has become a jungle. I hear waiters get lost from time to time. Why, just getting to the men's room makes me feel like Indiana Jones.

You get the point: They went a little overboard with the tropical decor. But this is a great-looking corner of Greenwich Village, animated by well-spiced Caribbean-Creole-West Indian cooking. The "Under $15" designation, however, does not budget for daiquiris, margaritas, and other exotic frozen drinks. At $3.75 a pop, some thirsty revelers spend over $15 on these alone. Portions are enormous, so don't get carried away with appetizers. This is the sort of advice I give but never follow. The fried okra, the conch fritters, and the mango chutney are superb.

The daily menu offers seventeen beef, chicken, goat, pork, and fish dishes, led by ropa vieja (shredded flank steak sautéed in spicy tomato sauce), chicken Caribe (baked in a medium-spicy sauce), picadillo (pork cubes in green peppers, onions, pimentos, and olives), and for heat-resistant palates, jerk chicken. Most are served with rice and either black beans or cabbage. Only fish entrees are priced over $8.95. It's probably best to go elsewhere for dessert—walk around the West Village and discover a cafe.

Carnegie Delicatessen & Restaurant

854 Seventh Ave., near 55th St.
Midtown West, Manhattan
757-2245
Open: seven days 6:30 A.M.–4 A.M.
By subway: B, D, E to 7th Ave.; N, Q, R to 57th St.
Average price per sandwich: $7.45
Alcohol: beer
Credit: none
Reservations: none
Classification: Positively NYC
Pièce de résistance: pastrami sandwich

Like its city, the Carnegie Deli is noisy, chaotic, overcrowded, excessive, and altogether one of the most exciting places to be on the planet. Several years ago my dad and I decided that our lunches together were too special to be held anywhere but this quintessential New York delicatessen. I'm sure that scores of other ladies and gents, including Carnegie's regular contingent of comedians and entertainers, feel the same way.

Prices may seem as bloated as the portions — a corned beef sandwich is $7.45 — but few leave disappointed. Carnegie's flavorful, nonkosher corned beef and pastrami sandwiches consistently measure up to their reputation as the biggest and best in town. Each is made with about three inches of the finest-quality meat, cured right on the premises. (Deluxe, combination, and club sandwiches are much thicker and virtually impossible to handle.) Ask for lean meat if that's your preference; it happens not to be mine. The clincher for any Carnegie sandwich is the fabulous, brick-oven baked rye bread.

Almost everything else I've tried at Carnegie, with the exception of the inexplicably boring French fries and home fries, caters to gluttons who can't get too much of a good thing. The extravagant breakfast-brunch fare is sensational: bagel platter with creamed cheese and lots of perfect nova; pastrami and eggs (delish!), corned beef hash, buttery French toast.

The only place to get any privacy at the Carnegie is in the rest rooms. Everyone dines at long, communal tables with little room for elbows or pastrami. I like this arrangement: You not only get to meet nice people, but you can see what they're having.

Carolina

1409 Mermaid Ave., near Stillwell Ave.
Coney Island, Brooklyn
(718) 266-8311
Open: Sun.–Thurs. noon–10 P.M., Fri. till 11 P.M., Sat. till
    midnight
By subway: B, D, F, N to Stillwell Ave.
Average price per entree: $7.50
Alcohol: beer and wine
Credit: none
Reservations: none
Classification: Ethnic Treasure
Pièce de résistance: saltimbocca alla Romana

Carolina is a cherished, neighborhood Italian restaurant for all of Brooklyn. It's the kind of place you go to with close friends or family on a Sunday night to be yourself and eat well. Unfortunately, there's not always enough room in Carolina's three pleasant dining rooms to accommodate the demand. Street lines outside Carolina are a Coney Island tradition.

Once seated, diners are treated to a free shot of vermouth and the waiting period is easily forgotten. A cold antipasto with lettuce, olives, celery, radishes, anchovies, cauliflower, egg, pickled eggplant, and carrots is probably the best start to an informal dinner, going nicely with fresh bread from a local bakery.

It's difficult to go wrong with anything on the menu. Simple homemade fettucine a filetto di pomodoro, with its zesty tomato sauce, typifies the fine quality of the pastas and sauces. Order it and the waiter may smile or wink at you because you're obviously among the cognoscenti. The saltimbocca alla Romana (veal scaloppine in wine sauce over a bed of spinach and topped with prosciutto and hard-boiled eggs) lives up to its name with a salty taste that "jumps into mouth." Chicken livers with mushrooms and onions may not be the most popular dish, but anyone who orders it is rewarded. The livers are not overcooked; the flavor is delightful. One seafood recommendation, calamari marinara, is as tender as you're likely to find.

Carolina serves a lovely bowl of assorted fruit for dessert, which is perhaps the most satisfying conclusion to a fine Italian dinner, followed by cappuccino or espresso and maybe a liqueur. By then, most diners are singing the praises of Carolina and planning a return visit to Coney Island.

Chez Brigitte

77 Greenwich Ave., near Seventh Ave.
Greenwich Village, Manhattan
929-6736
Open: Mon.–Sat. 11 A.M.–9 P.M.
By subway: 1, 2, 3 to 14th St.
Average price per entree: $6
Alcohol: none
Credit: none
Reservations: none
Classification: Wholesome Hideaway
Pièce de résistance: veal cutlet sandwich

An American alone and flustered in Paris would find a snug refuge like Chez Brigitte as inviting as the scent of soupe a l'oignon. As it happens, this petite luncheonette resides in a city where its charms are needed most. The tiny, French-accented shop seats eleven lucky West Villagers and stands no more than two—sometimes warm-hearted Brigitte and her helper—to prepare and serve meals and refreshments.

Invigorating lunches and dinners, modest in scope, abundant in love, include beef bourguignon, leg of lamb, chicken fricassee, roast pork, and a selection of hero sandwiches on French bread. Best of those is the veal cutlet sprinkled with lemon. There are also soups, omelets, and homemade pies which, though unexceptional, are irresistible, if only to prolong your stay. Same goes for a second cup of coffee (or glass of iced coffee during the summer). Brigitte and her devotees take coffee very seriously.

Chez Laurence Patisserie

245 Madison Ave., at 38th St.
Midtown East, Manhattan
683-0284
Open: Mon.–Fri. 7 A.M.–6:30 P.M.
By subway: 4, 5, 6, 7, S to Grand Central
Average price per pastry: $2.50
Alcohol: none
Credit: none
Reservations: none
Classification: Wholesome Hideaway
Pièce de résistance: the Eggspresso

Bohemians in business suits loosen their ties and free their reveries at Chez Laurence, a delightful French cafe and patisserie on the first floor of the Madison Towers Hotel. The decor itself inspires the imagination: Likenesses of Charlie Chaplin, Greta Garbo, and Ingrid Bergman look down from magnificent French movie posters to a roomful of marble-topped tables and walnut captain's chairs. Though situated at 38th and Madison in midtown, the place ought to have a Greenwich Village zip code.

The selection of crusty croissants, brioches, and fine pastries is wonderful. I especially like the apple tart, the feuillette aux fraises (a puffed pastry with custard and strawberries), or anything chocolate. Their soup and sandwich combinations ($3.25–$4) make splendid lunches. Sandwiches are prepared on handmade whole wheat, pumpernickel, or rye. My pick is the mackerel and grated carrot salad sandwich. Believe me, mackerel does a lot more for carrot salad than raisins.

Chez Laurence can get a little too busy for comfort during lunch hours. Stop by, if you can, after three in the afternoon or anytime in the morning for one of two worthwhile breakfast specials (7–10 A.M.): the Eggspresso (two fluffy "cappuccino" scrambled eggs, croissant or brioche, confiture, coffee or tea; $2.95) or the same without eggs ($1.95).

Christine's

208 First Ave., near 12th St.
East Village, Manhattan
505-0376
Open: seven days 6 A.M.–10 P.M.
By subway: L to 1st Ave.
Average price per order of blintzes: $3.25
Alcohol: beer

438 Second Ave., at 25th St.
Kips Bay, Manhattan
684-1878

Open: seven days 7 A.M.–10 P.M.
By subway: 6 to 23rd St.
Average price per order of blintzes: $3.25
Alcohol: beer and wine

344 Lexington Ave., near 40th St.
Midtown East, Manhattan
953-1920
Open: seven days 11 A.M.–9 P.M.
By subway: 4, 5, 6, 7, S to Grand Central
Average price per order of blintzes: $5.25
Alcohol: beer and wine

Credit: none
Reservations: none
Classification: Ethnic Treasure
Pièce de résistance: white borscht soup

Loyalty is taken to extremes at Christine's, now a chain of three Polish restaurants that have taken over the East Side of Manhattan. Some regulars at the original, newly expanded coffee shop on First Avenue drop in for three meals a day. Here's how I'd do it: banana pancakes or challah French toast for breakfast; one of the fabulous soups (definitely white borscht with kielbasa and boiled potato if it's the soup of the day) and a plate of cheese blintzes or boiled potato pierogi for lunch; breaded breast of chicken cutlet (it doesn't get more tender or juicy than this) with sides of red cabbage and home fries for dinner. And somewhere in between there I'd sneak back in a fourth time for a wedge of toasted babka and coffee.

The Princess of Pierogi does change her clothes a little as she moves uptown. The First Avenue location, on the East Village's Blintz Belt, is an austere coffee shop—nothing to look at but lots of great smells and tastes. Its Second Avenue counterpart is a little nicer, resembling a typical Manhattan diner. The Midtown location, however, is a comfortable, modestly elegant restaurant with such modern details as glass tops over the tablecloths, track lighting, a neon specials board, and somewhat higher prices.

You can still eat a solid home-style Polish dinner for well under $15 at the dressier Christine's, for under $10 at the two coffee shops. That's cause for solidarity.

Country Life

48 Trinity Pl., at Rector St.
Financial District, Manhattan
480-9135
Open: breakfast Mon.–Fri. 7:30 A.M.–9:15 A.M.,
    lunch 11:15 A.M.–2:30 P.M.
By subway: 1, R to Rector St.; 4, 5 to Wall St.

244 East 51st St., near Second Ave.
Midtown East, Manhattan
980-1595
Open: lunch Mon.–Fri. 11:30 A.M.–2:30 P.M., dinner
    Sun.–Thurs. 6 P.M.–8 P.M.
By subway: 6 to 51st St.; E, F to Lexington Ave.

Price per buffet: lunch $5.95, dinner $7.39
Alcohol: none
Credit: none
Reservations: none
Classification: Wholesome Hideaway
Pièce de résistance: harvest nut roast

Country Life is a restaurant with a mission: to nourish New Yorkers and expose them to the creative possibilities of cooking without meats, eggs, or dairy. Both locations are owned and operated by laymen of the health-minded Seventh-Day Adventist Church. Don't dare let that intimidate you. Guests are not greeted by any kind of religious solicitations. There's just a friendly grocery store and an all-you-can-eat buffet. The lunch spread offers one hot entree, vegetables, rice, salad bar, fruit bar, whole-grain breads, and nut spreads — peanut, hazelnut, and almond butter.

Country Life is a vegetarian restaurant intent upon pleasing nonvegetarians. Their adaptations of favorite ethnic dishes might astonish if not excite you. Lasagna is prepared with two nondairy "cheeses": one of tofu and the other with tahini and pimentos. Enchiladas, also made with a nondairy cheese, are spiced with garlic and cumin rather than hot peppers that can irritate the stomach. Harvest nut roast, which resembles turkey stuffing, is made with bread crumbs, pecans, sunflower seeds, celery, onions, and a cashew-based gravy.

The food is basically the same at the two Country Lifes, but choose, if convenient, the newer, more attractive, uptown location. Situated in an East Side townhouse, the lovely, two-tiered dining room has the feel of a woodsy northern California retreat, an atmosphere the wholesome foods only reinforce.

The downtown location's breakfast buffet includes a hot entree, hot and cold cereals, dry and fresh fruits, muffins, and Danish. You can eat all you want for only $3.49.

Call the recorded-menu hotline at 480-9142 for the specials of the day.

Cucina Stagionale

275 Bleecker St., at Jones St.
Greenwich Village, Manhattan
924-2707
Open: seven days noon–midnight
By subway: 1 to Christopher St.; A, B, C, D, E, F, Q to West 4th St.
Average price per pasta: $6
Alcohol: none
Credit: none
Reservations: none
Classification: Ethnic Treasure
Pièce de résistance: spinach penne with seasonal vegetables, sun-dried tomatoes, and fontina cheese

Cucina di Pesce

87 East 4th St., near Second Ave.
East Village, Manhattan
260-6800
Open: Mon.–Sat. 5 P.M.–midnight, Sun. 4 P.M.–11 P.M.
By subway: 6 to Astor Pl.; F to Second Ave.
Alcohol: yes
Credit: none
Reservations: none
Classification: Ethnic Treasure
Pièce de résistance: broiled bluefish

Good things come to those who wait at Cucina Stagionale, an Italian restaurant that's lovely to look at, delightful to know. Cucina's dainty decor and prized pastas take "Under $15" restaurantgoers out of their milieu but not out of their budget. This all may sound too good to be true and it is. Long lines form outside the restaurant nearly every night. But the wait can be avoided by coming in for lunch or an early dinner before 5:30 P.M.

Each appetizer is a work of art, using a palette of the freshest ingredients. Two extraordinary examples: strawberry and pesto salad with endive and mozzarella on a bed of radicchio; marinated baked eggplant and roasted pepper with provolone, smoked mozzarella, and sun-dried tomatoes. These appetizing excursions are $3.95 apiece, a bargain surpassed only by the thirteen $5.95 to $6.95 pasta dishes.

Consider conchiglie with sautéed calamari in spicy red sauce; spinach penne with seasonal vegetables, sun-dried tomatoes, and fontina cheese; fusilli with sun-dried tomatoes, gorgonzola, and capers in cream sauce; eggplant manicotti with enriched ricotta cheese . . . need I go on? These are life-enhancing pastas and sauces. Cucina also features veal, chicken, and fresh fish and seafood specials ($7.95 to $11.95) and some enticing desserts.

The fifty-seat dining room is homelike and Laura Ashley-esque, with pink tablecloths and a variety of plates, prints, and wall hangings. It's all very nice, yet secondary once the gratis cold antipasto and crusty Italian bread arrive.

Cucina Stagionale now has a younger sister residing in the East Village, Cucina di Pesce. Its decor is more old-world, but the food and prices are every bit as good and the selection of fish, naturally, is much better. A stirring example is broiled bluefish in a sauce of marsala wine, sun-dried tomatoes, sautéed garlic, orange peel, and almonds, served with a bowl of pasta marinara, for just $8.95.

Cucina di Pesce has a lovely bar area, which may be a plus or a minus, depending on your perspective. It provides a place to relax while you wait for a table, but pennywise patrons like myself cannot bring their own bottle of wine. No one seems to mind waiting, though. Tortellini and mussels or calamari marinara are served at the bar.

Dagon Burmese

557 Hudson St., near West 11th St.
Greenwich Village, Manhattan
206-0660
Open: Sun.–Thurs. noon–11 P.M., Fri. & Sat. till
    midnight
By subway: 1 to Christopher St.; A, C, E to 14th St.
Average price per entree: $7
Alcohol: beer and wine
Credit: AE
Reservations: not necessary
Classification: Ethnic Treasure
Pièce de résistance: coconut milk beef curry with
    potatoes

It's not going to happen. Burmese will not be the next fashionable ethnic cuisine you read all about in the trend-setting magazines. But its primary public relations problem—the all-too-frequent comparisons to Indian, Thai, and Chinese cooking—may be what you like best about it.

Dagon Burmese is a pleasant neighborhood place serving food that is at once strange and familiar. The dishes are new to most of us but the ingredients and many of their combinations are certainly not. Several of the chicken, beef, pork, or shrimp specialties are prepared with either curry or green pepper, sliced onion, and tomato.

Recommended appetizers include the gold fingers (fried calabash sticks) or golden triangles (potatoes wrapped in thin pastry and fried), both served with hot pepper dip, or pork rolls (sautéed shredded pork, egg, cabbage, and scallion wrapped in a roll and steamed). Though none of the main courses I've tried are standouts, I would suggest the coconut milk beef curry with potatoes (served in a round bowl), pepper duck (a colorful plate of boneless duck sautéed with green and red pepper and lemon grass in wine sauce), and, when in season, prawn and asparagus (stir-fried with green pepper in a light garlic sauce). Rangoon night market noodles (like duck lo mein) should be avoided; even the name suggests immorality.

Best of the coconut desserts is the warm, multi-layered pancake topped with an ultrasweet coconut milk topping.

Dallas BBQ

27 West 72nd St., near Central Park West
Upper West Side, Manhattan
873-2004
Open: Sun.–Thurs. noon–midnight, Fri. & Sat. till
   1 A.M.
By subway: 1, 2, 3, C to 72nd St.
Average price per entree: $7
Alcohol: yes
Credit: AE, DC, MC, V
Reservations: none
Classification: A Little Romance
Pièce de résistance: chicken & ribs combo

New York is not a great rib town, which is probably why a place like this needs a name like Dallas BBQ. There is actually an establishment on the Upper East Side called the Great Manhattan Rib and Chicken Co., an oxymoron comparable to, say, the Great Biloxi Bagel and Lox Co.

Dallas BBQ does live up to its name in sheer size. This is a lofty and comfortable if noisy place to dine at deflated prices. The barbecue is neither spicy nor smokey, yet the charred baby back ribs are tender and tasty enough and the chicken is done right. A combo plate, including corn bread and baked or French-fried potatoes, is $8.95; a half-chicken plate is $4.95. Texas-sized appetites may prefer the meatier barbecued beef ribs over the pork ribs.

The most popular side order/appetizer is the enormous onion loaf. Digging into that brick of deep-fried batter and onions is a little too much like striking oil at the dinner table. It's not for everybody. Dallas BBQ also features a remarkable early-bird special from noon to 6:30 P.M. Monday through Saturday: two chicken vegetable soups, two half-chickens, corn bread, and potatoes for $6.95 per couple. That's right, a half-penny less than $3.48 per person.

Deninos

524 Richmond Ave., at Hooker Pl.
Port Richmond, Staten Island
(718) 442-9401
Open: seven days 11:30 A.M.–12:30 A.M.
Average price per large pizza: $6.75
Alcohol: yes
Credit: none
Reservations: none
Classification: Ethnic Treasure
Pièce de résistance: ricotta cheese pizza

Ralph's Ices

501 Richmond Ave., at Catherine St.
Port Richmond, Staten Island
(718) 273-3675
Open: seven days noon–11 P.M. (summer only)
Average price per ice: $1
Classification: Positively NYC
Pièce de résistance: lemon Italian ices

As someone who's always hungry for a new New York adventure, I thought it would be a good idea to take a date of mine on a journey to Staten Island. We traveled under land, over sea, and over land for a classic one-two punch in summer eating: Deninos' pizza and Ralph's Italian ices. Unfortunately, she did not appreciate the ninety-minute subway-ferry-bus trip back and forth or the man who dragged her through it. I never saw or heard from her again.

Sure, it takes some kind of certified nut to make a trip like that just for pizza and ices, but I see it as an excuse to take the ferry and visit the forgotten borough.

Deninos is a nondescript, red-brick tavern just beyond the shadow of the Bayonne Bridge. Hidden from the bar and pool table up front is a dark dining room where crispy-crust lovers leer at the kitchen door, waiting for the entrance of another classic pie. These are beautiful pizzas with extra-fresh extras (think hard about having the ricotta cheese pie) and an all-city crust. I wouldn't dream of leaving behind a crust end.

Across the avenue, Ralph's drive-in serves up priceless Italian ices. The first lick from a cup of Ralph's homemade ices is one of the great thrills of summer, thanks to their sweet, rich flavorings and their perfectly smooth consistency. The jewel of Ralph's six-flavor palette is lemon, which is made with fresh lemons, even though the product has a short freezer life. Honorable mention goes to the others: chocolate, watermelon, pineapple, cherry, and orange.

Ralph's was opened in 1949 by the late Ralph Silvestro and is now run by his daughters and grandsons. Family members constantly try to top each other by developing new flavors of creme ice, a house specialty made with cream and milk. Among the lasting successes: piña colada, cappuccino, chocolate chip, and cremalata.

Deninos ricotta pizza, Ralph's lemon ices, the Staten Island ferry . . . I could but didn't fall in love on an evening such as this.

Ecco-La

1660 Third Ave., at East 93rd St.
Upper East Side, Manhattan
860-5609
Open: Sun. noon–10:30 P.M., Mon.–Thurs. till
    11:30 P.M., Fri. & Sat. till midnight
By subway: 6 to 96th St.
Average price per pasta: $7.95
Alcohol: yes
Credit: none
Reservations: none
Classification: Funky Casual
Pièce de résistance: capelli Marina

A better name for this nouvelle pasta place would've been Echo-La. It's so noisy inside, the waitstaff and diners need to learn sign language. This is not done because people could really hurt themselves trying to sign Pappardella Della Nonna Debora.

The clatter inside and outside Ecco-La, however, is very much a part of the new vibrancy of upper Third Avenue and the excitement surrounding a good, chic, inexpensive place to eat.

Most everything on Ecco-La's menu of eight antipasti, $3.95 to $4.95, and eighteen pastas, $6.95 to $8.95, all beautifully plated, would entice any Under $15 fanatic or Over $40 wanna-be. The Insalada Papi, for example, is a wonderful mix of endive, radicchio, avocado, roasted peppers, onions, watercress, artichokes, and tomatoes. Capelli Marina, angel hair pasta with a seafood sauce of mussels, white fish, shrimp, and lobster in a light tomato cream sauce, is sensational. The kitchen does overextend itself a little and slips on occasion, but these are minor.

Ecco-La has a funky, contemporary look with striped pillars that look like giant packs of Life Savers. The wait for a table can be up to an hour, so come before 7 P.M. if you want to avoid the crowds.

By the way, the lyrically named Pappardella Della Nonna Debora is wide pasta ribbons with wild mushrooms, marsala wine, sun-dried tomatoes, garlic, and parmesan.

Eddie's Sweet Shop

105-29 Metropolitan Ave., at 72nd Rd.
Forest Hills, Queens
(718) 520-8514
Open: Tues.–Fri. 1 P.M.–11:30 P.M., Sat. & Sun. noon–
    11:30 P.M.
By subway: E, F, G, R to 71st–Continental Aves., then
    Q23 bus to Metropolitan Ave.
Average price per sundae: $3
Alcohol: none
Credit: none
Reservations: none
Classification: A Little Romance
Pièce de résistance: banana split

The glory days of Eddie's Sweet Shop, the old-fashioned ice cream parlor in Forest Hills, are now. On summer Saturday nights, a team of soda jerks works frantically to satisfy a steady flow of movie-goers from the Cinemart Twin down the block. Sentimentalists bring their dates or families to get more for their ice cream fantasies than a cone and a napkin.

Eddie's, like a new print of an old movie, is a living classic. Its precious fixtures—marble counter, mahogany back bar, wooden stools with brass footstops, ornate woodwork, tiled floor, tin ceiling—evoke a sublime promise: romantic Saturday nights with dreamy sundaes and sodas, all made with homemade ice cream.

Eddie's rich, creamy, superpremium ice cream comes in seventeen flavors (the most exotic is pistachio pineapple). In addition, there's a choice of seven toppings and ten syrups to further customize the sundaes and sodas. The latter are prepared extra-sweet. The banana split ($3.40) is misnamed; no one has ever willingly shared it.

Eisenberg Sandwich Shop

174 Fifth Ave., near West 22nd St.
Flatiron District, Manhattan
675-5096
By subway: N, R to 23rd St.
Average price per sandwich: $2.50
Alcohol: none
Credit: none
Reservations: none
Classification: Positively NYC
Pièce de résistance: tuna sandwich

A romanticized view of New York's good ol' days is borne out by a visit to Eisenberg Sandwich Shop. The old-fashioned luncheonette is situated, appropriately, across from the Flatiron Building, the 1902 triangular skyscraper whose very sight mesmerizes many New Yorkers. Eisenberg's can have a similar effect. Stepping inside the shop, with its long marble counter, soft lighting, high ceiling, and dated fixtures, is like walking into an Edward Hopper painting.

The mood is only enhanced by the friendly, gracious service. The owners and help live by the message taped to the cash register: "It's nice to be important, but it's more important to be nice." During one visit I asked the jolly counterman, Walter, who does not know that I am a food writer, for some more hot water in my teacup (I'll do anything to delay my departure). He took the cup, turned his back to me, and tried to conceal the fact that he was giving me a new tea bag. This small gesture of anonymous giving best explains why a whipped, white tuna sandwich, a toasted bagel with creamed cheese, poached eggs on toast, a soda served in a paper cone, or any other routine breakfast or lunch item seems to taste better at Eisenberg's. They're prepared by people who care.

El Pollo

1746 First Ave. near East 91st St.
Upper East Side, Manhattan
996-7810
Open: Mon.–Fri. 11:30 A.M.–11 P.M., Sat. & Sun.
    12:30 P.M.–11 P.M.

By subway: 4, 5, 6 to 86th St.
Average price per dinner: $7
Alcohol: none
Credit: none
Reservations: none
Classification: Ethnic Treasure
Pièce de résistance: Peruvian-style barbecued chicken

Lucio Medina, El Pollo's spin doctor, has set a new standard for rotisserie chicken. His Peruvian-style barbecued chicken, marinated overnight in garlic, soy sauce, vinegar, paprika, white wine, salt, ginger, oregano, white pepper, and two secret spices, explodes with juice and flavor all the way down to the bone. On the local chicken charts, El Pollo is a pullet with a bullet.

Each order of succulent chicken ($2.25 for a quarter; $3.70 for a half) is served with two dipping sauces: a green sauce of jalapeño pepper and the Peruvian herb huacatay that could burn a hole through concrete and a milder white sauce of sour cream, huacatay, and a hint of hot pepper.

Among the splendid sides: fresh curly fries, papa rellena, which is like a deep-fried potato knish stuffed with ground meat, egg, and pepper, and mote (Peruvian corn).

The narrow shop, which has both table and take-out service, is casual and cute, with an exposed-brick wall, new tin ceiling, three ceiling fans spinning shadows, and any number of happy chicken lovers.

El Sombrero

108 Stanton St., at Ludlow St.
Lower East Side, Manhattan
254-4188
Open: seven days noon–midnight
By subway: F to Delancey St.; J, M to Essex St.
Average price per entree: $7
Alcohol: beer and margaritas
Credit: none
Reservations: none
Classification: Ethnic Treasure
Pièce de résistance: budin Azteca

El Sombrero, or to its friends, "The Hat," is tacky, lowbrow, positively déclassé. I felt I ought to tell you that before talking you into going. For this is the sort of honest, homestyle Mexican restaurant that New Yorkers are demanding now that many of the flashy, noisy, pricey, Mexican "bars" uptown have lost their novelty. Situated one block south of Katz's Deli on the Lower East Side, the Hat draws more East Villagers than an ad for a $250 apartment.

You can taste the incentive for this nightly, southward migration in fresh, rich tomato and chili sauces and well-marinated meats. The meat is so good in the chicken fajita, for example, that you may want to put the tortilla down and give each individual chunk the attention and appreciation it deserves.

Likewise, I find it necessary to slow down while eating the budin Azteca, which is described as a Mexican quiche, but is more like a cheese-

and-tortilla casserole with green chili sauce. Some other tips of the Hat to the tostada del mar (with seafood) and the carnitas (shredded pork sautéed with orange and pineapple). Entrees are mostly $6 to $7.50; $3 appetizers like the quesadillas (cheese-filled fried tortillas topped with salsa and guaca-mole) and the nachos provide fabulous accompaniment for the frozen margaritas.

Empire Diner

210 Tenth Ave, at West 22nd St.
Chelsea, Manhattan
243-2736
Open: seven days 24 hours
By subway: C, E to 23rd St.
Average price per sandwich plate: $7.50
Alcohol: yes
Credit: AE
Reservations: none
Classification: Positively NYC
Pièce de résistance: "today's hedonist sandwich"

The Empire Diner looks and feels great on us. This icon of Art Deco, with its glossy black-and-chrome interior, sends urban romantics soaring as effortlessly as a favorite black-and-white movie. It's where Fred Astaire and Ginger Rogers would've gone for breakfast after a long night of club hopping.

Nearly everything on the menu seems overpriced as diner fare—a plate of bacon and eggs is $5.25—but I prefer to view it all as affordable fantasy. Such daily sandwiches as turkey club and avocado or bacon and Swiss are quite good; the "hedonist's" sandwich of the day is usually a mouth-watering combo. A few examples: avocado, roast beef, and melted swiss on rye bread; Moroccan lamb (ground lamb and spinach in pita); Le Hot Dog (grilled knockwurst and melted Swiss on French bread); smoked mozzarella, sliced tomato, pesto mayonnaise on French bread. One regular, rocker/actress Debbie Harry, loves the soups. I'm into the French toast. One way or another, they're gonna getcha.

Tables with umbrellas are set up on the sidewalk during warm-weather months, but you still may prefer to stay indoors, listen to the pianist play Cole Porter, and see the reflection of a dream in the Empire Diner's shiny tabletops.

Exterminator Chili

305 Church St., south of Canal St.
TriBeCa, Manhattan
219-3070
Open: Mon.–Thurs. 7:30 A.M.–4 P.M. & 6 P.M.–11 P.M.,
  Fri. till midnight, Sat. & Sun. 11 A.M.–11 P.M.
By subway: A, C, E to Canal St.
Average price per entree: $8
Alcohol: yes
Credit: none
Reservations: none
Classification: Funky Casual
Pièce de résistance: industrial chili

Some would call it chance. I say fate made Steve Frankel gaze out his bathroom window that summer morning. Outside, the billboard read: "Exterminator: Residential, Commercial, Industrial, Agricultural." It was a divine inspiration, not to fumigate his apartment, but to open Exterminator Chili, a downtown hotspot serving four grades of chili that get the job done.

Personally, I question the wisdom of linking such a likeable eating establishment with pest control. The whimsical interior resembles a typical diner hastily and elaborately decorated for a Tex-Mex theme party. Novelties you'd expect to find in a San Antonio gift shop – a neon oil well, a photo of Roy Rogers and Trigger, a clock made from the (hit?) single "Moon Lite Chili" – adorn the stuccoed walls. The room is lined with red and green Christmas lights which, if you've never noticed, are shaped like jalapeño peppers.

Despite the menacing name, even the Industrial (hottest grade) chili will not scorch your gums, intestines, or points between. You might sweat a little (no more than after a half hour of paddleball), but those who eat to suffer will be disappointed. The lure is the imaginative and ever-expanding collection of chili recipes that are rotated. An example of Commercial (medium-hot grade) was prepared with large chunks of turkey and Mexican green tomatoes. Splendid! An Industrial, made with ham and toasted, dried chili pepper, was thick and richly flavored. A mild Residential consisting of ground beef and chorizo was lively yet temperate.

Each chili is served in a bowl over black beans and rice, topped with onions, shredded cheddar, and sour cream, and accompanied by tortilla chips and red or green cole slaw. The price is $6 for lunch; $8 for dinner. Also offered are burgers, sandwiches, salads, thick shakes, and homemade desserts.

Ferdinando's Foccoceria

151 Union St., near Hicks Dr.
Carroll Gardens, Brooklyn
(718) 855-1545
Open: Mon.–Sat. 9:30 A.M.–5 P.M.
By subway: F, G to Carroll St.
Average price per main course: $5
Alcohol: beer and wine
Credit: none
Reservations: none
Classification: Ethnic Treasure
Pièce de résistance: panelle with ricotta cheese

"You're living in the past," the realist tells his friend the Brooklyn romantic. "The Dodgers left town thirty years ago and so did all that was special about Brooklyn."

"Phooey," responds the romantic, who immediately heads down Union Street towards Ferdinando's Foccoceria. At that quiet shop on a quiet street in a quiet neighborhood in Brooklyn, anachronism is honored, not ridiculed. The romantic sits down in the quaint, seventy-five-year-old eatery, rests his feet on the antique tile floor, looks around at the checkered tablecloths, tin ceiling, and brick walls, and knows he's found his time and place.

And nothing reinforces those feelings of belonging and acceptance like the Italian morsels cooked up at Ferdinando's. One bite of a hot panelle (chick-pea bread fried in olive oil) topped with ricotta cheese is a swoonful. Likewise the rice ball with ricotta. And how about those midday main courses! The bracciola alla contadina (beef rolled with eggs, bread crumbs, onion, black pep-

per, white wine, and grated Romano cheese and
then baked) and eggplant parmigiana, both in a
lightly peppered tomato sauce, are prepared to such
delicate perfection that you might fear injury to the
food by using a knife and fork. And now there's a
new specialty at Ferdinando's: sun-dried tomatoes
stuffed with bread crumbs, garlic, olive oil, black
pepper, and red pepper, then fried in olive oil and
served with eggplant salad.

After lunch, the romantic's first inclination is to
take his friend the realist to Ferdinando's the next
day. A moment later he decides against it. Some
things in life, he concludes, should be reserved for
true believers.

Flor de Mayo

2651 Broadway, near West 101st St.
Upper West Side, Manhattan
663-5520
By subway: 1 to 103rd St.
Alcohol: beer

2282 Broadway, near West 82nd St.
Upper West Side, Manhattan
595-2525
By subway: 1 to 79th St.
Alcohol: none

Open: Seven days, noon–midnight
Average price per entree: $6.50
Credit: none
Reservations: none
Classification: Ethnic Treasure
Pièce de résistance: picadillo

The original Flor de Mayo at 82nd and Broadway, like most of the more popular Chinese-Latino places around town, gets a good-great-poor rating: good food, great prices, poor ambiance. Fortunately, they moved just the first two-thirds of that rating one mile north when they opened the refreshingly clean and contemporary Flor de Mayo II at West 101st St.

Part of the new look consists of seventeen Hong Kong–style dishes to go along with the standard Cuban and Cantonese menu. Still, I recommend you first try such Cuban standbys as ropa vieja (shredded beef Cuban style), picadillo (chopped beef Cuban style), or pollo asado (broiled chicken), all served with white or yellow rice and black beans and priced from $5 to $6.55. Nice additions are fried plantains and the sliced avocado salad with onions and fresh lemon. One Hong Kong dish I especially enjoyed was king do gai, as much for the sweet-and-sour dipping sauce, which I spooned over the white rice, as the tender, crisp-edged fried chicken nuggets. Next time in, however, I went back to picadillo.

The new Flor de Mayo's too-bright, split-level dining room is attractively furnished with black laminate tables with solid-oak borders, a polished parquet floor, mauve walls, and an aquarium. Service at both branches is always relaxed and friendly.

Gefen's

297 Seventh Ave., near 27th St.
Garment Center, Manhattan
929-6476
Open: Mon.–Thurs. 6 A.M.–8 P.M., Fri. till 2 P.M., Sun.
    1 P.M.–8 P.M.
By subway: 1 to 28th St.
Average price per lunch entree: $7
Alcohol: none
Credit: none
Reservations: none
Classification: Wholesome Hideaway
Pièce de résistance: Hungarian goulash

Hotshot garment industry types can be reduced to quivering indecision at Gefen's, a superb kosher dairy restaurant opposite the Fashion Institute of Technology. Ordering, say, eggplant steak means rejecting mamma's blintzes. They can't do it. There's just too much good home cooking to choose from, so they overeat.

Here are some pointers to assist the undecided, all good, honest people who want only something nice to eat:

1. It's not kosher to skip the hearty soup of the day. I'd have a bowl of split pea or mushroom and barley on the hottest day of the year.
2. Think kasha varnishkes (buckwheat groats and bowtie noodles) with onion gravy and creamed spinach. Order them as your entire lunch or work them in as side attractions to a larger program.
3. Don't think of the vegetarian Hungarian goulash or the eggplant steak as meat substitutes. They stand up on their own.

4. Take an early train in the morning and stop in for the challah French toast for breakfast. But insist that the man behind the counter soak the bread well before throwing it on the griddle.

Gefen's contemporary decor is pleasant enough, though hardly distinctive. All the character this place needs comes from its wholesome food and the colorful people who consume it.

Good Enough to Eat

424 Amsterdam Ave., near West 80th St.
Upper West Side, Manhattan
496-0163
Open for breakfast: Mon.–Fri. 8 A.M.–4 P.M., Sat. & Sun. 9 A.M.–4 P.M.
By subway: 1 to 79th St.
Average price per breakfast: $7
Alcohol: none
Credit: none
Reservations: none
Classification: Wholesome Hideaway
Pièce de résistance: lumber jack

Good Enough to Eat is a rather modest description for the hearty, country breakfasts prepared at this cozy little oasis on the Upper West Side. There's often a prohibitively long wait for a table on weekends; come on a weekday morning if you can, when all is quiet and civilized. I've noticed that more and more creative businesspeople are coming in for breakfast meetings. The quaint atmosphere seems to suit them; negotiations flourish when the aroma of cooking slab bacon is in the air.

The dining area is small, with about ten mix 'n' match country block and sewing machine tables, a brick wall, and homespun wallpaper and wall hangings. It's an appropriate setting for people who take breakfast seriously and are not accustomed to finishing their morning meal in eight minutes or less.

The menu, appealing from top to bottom, features the lumber jack (two pancakes, three strips of slab bacon, two scrambled eggs; the farm house (two poached eggs on grilled dill-onion bread with patty sausages); cinnamon swirl French toast (topped with cinnamon, sugar, cocoa, raisins, and nuts); banana walnut pancakes; and pecan waffles. Most are accompanied by fine jams and delicious strawberry butter.

Since pancake houses are just about extinct in Manhattan, Good Enough to Eat has become the place to go for a stack. They're soft but not too fluffy and served with pure maple syrup.

Grand Dairy

341 Grand St., at Ludlow St.
Lower East Side, Manhattan
673-1904
Open: Sun.–Fri. 6 A.M.–3:30 P.M.
By subway: B, D, Q to Grand St.; F to Delancy St.; J, M to Essex St.
Average price per lunch item: $4
Alcohol: none
Credit: none
Reservations: none
Classification: Ethnic Treasure
Pièce de résistance: soup du jour

Is nothing sacred anymore? The Ludlow Street bachelor's most faithful relationship—with the understanding potato soup at Grand Dairy—is kaput. I was the hungry reporter who broke the story in the New York *Daily News*. I spotted him at Grand Dairy's counter one Wednesday with a bowl of cabbage soup, followed by a monstrous salmon cutlet and rice pudding. He also finished a basket of fresh Russian black bread, pumpernickel, and assorted rolls. What an appetite! No wonder he's lonely.

Grand Dairy does a commendable job with its vast selection of Jewish-style meatless specialties, among them kasha blintzes, western omelet with lox, chopped egg and celery sandwich, mushroom cutlet, strawberries with sour cream, and scrambled eggs and onions (the last is close to my heart). Nothing, however, approaches the goodness of their stocky homemade soups—green or yellow split pea, potato, mushroom barley, cabbage, vegetable, and Yankee bean—accompanied by the fresh black bread.

For dessert, the baked rice pudding (Mondays and Wednesdays only) and noodle pudding (Sundays, Tuesdays, and Thursdays), each topped with a hot, sweetened, pineapple-cherry fruit sauce, are classics. If you prefer the hardened, slightly burned edges bordering the pan, ask for a corner piece. Softies should demand a center square. Similar rules apply to a square of chunky apple cake.

The best that can be said about the interior of Grand Dairy is that it can't be as dirty as it looks.

Still, most of the twenty-odd tables-for-four fill up at lunchtime, making it apparent that everyone, whether sleek or slovenly, loved or lonely, likes to be coddled by a hearty bowl of soup.

Hamburger Harry's

145 West 45th St., near Seventh Ave.
Theater District, New York
840-2756
Open: seven days 11:30 A.M.–11 P.M.
By subway: B, D, F to 42nd St.; 1, 2, 3, 7, R, N, Q to Times Square.

157 Chambers St., near Greenwich St.
Financial District, Manhattan
267-4446
Open: Sun.–Thurs. 11:30 A.M.–11:30 P.M., Fri. & Sat. till midnight
By subway: 1, 2, 3, A, C, E to Chambers St.

Average price per burger: $4
Alcohol: yes
Credit: AE
Reservations: not necessary
Classification: Funky Casual
Pièce de résistance: béarnaise burger

Don't think of Hamburger Harry's as just a couple of burger joints. New York's ground-meat maven operates two sleek, steel-blue showcases for America's favorite sandwich. Like going to the dentist, you'll have to open wide for their mammoth, mesquite-grilled burgers with a variety of topnotch toppings, from béarnaise sauce to chili. For the truly shameless there's the Ha Ha burger, topped with chili, cheddar, onion, guacamole, and pico de gallo sauce. But any way you top it, this is a great burger: seven ounces of just-lean-enough meat, grilled to near perfection and served on a sesame-seed bun with a leaf of romaine lettuce and a slice of tomato. Have a side order of Ha Ha's curly French fries and you're all set.

The newer Ha Ha's near Times Square, like the original downtown location, is an upbeat update on 1950s-diner modern. The two dining levels are strategically arranged with red chairs and wood tables. A long oval ceiling fixture, trimmed with fluorescent light, extends to the U-shaped counter in the rear. From there, you get a view of the partially exposed kitchen, where charcoal and mesquite wood are always ablaze, ready to char Ha Ha's round mounds of renown.

Harry's Burritos

91 East 7th St., near First Ave.
East Village, Manhattan
477-0773
Open: Sun.–Thurs. noon–midnight, Fri. & Sat. till 2 A.M.
By subway: 6 to Astor Pl.
Alcohol: none

Benny's Burritos

113 Greenwich Ave., at Jane St.
Greenwich Village, Manhattan
633-9210

Open: seven days noon–midnight
By subway: 1, 2, 3, A, C, E to 14th St.;
   L to Eighth Ave.
Alcohol: beer

Average price per entree: $4.75
Credit: none
Reservations: none
Classification: Funky Casual
Pièce de résistance: mission burrito

I think Harry is insecure. He obviously feels it is
necessary to compensate for his tiny restaurant by
wrapping large quantities of beans, rice, cheese,
guacamole, chicken, beef, or whatever into jumbo,
twelve-inch tortilla pouches. At Harry's, you can
stretch your body but not your legs.

Luckily, Harry realizes that size is not everything. His two-handed burritos ($3.75 to $4.75) are
made with fresh, mostly top-shelf ingredients and
no salt overdoses. The meatless mission burrito is a
powerhouse of beans, rice, cheese, guacamole, and
sour cream. Similar to but lighter than the burritos
is the soft taco Dolores ($3), which is made with a
corn tortilla rather than one of flour. The taco,
filled with beef, black beans, and cheese and served
with lettuce, tomato, and salsa (actually chopped
fresh tomatoes sprinkled with cilantro), is simply
delicious. Add an appetizer of good-quality guacamole and a soda and you've got a complete meal-
on-the-move for $5.35.

The shop itself, though too small for a game of
solitaire, is a fun hangout with personality —
nothing like the assembly line, high-tech, fast-food

salt palaces on the avenues. To my mind, the city can't have too many places like it.

Benny's brings the taste and flavor of Harry's to the West Village. It's a larger store than the original, but nothing in the kitchen or the mood has been compromised. Most tables are at or near the high windows, providing a panoramic view of the comings and goings along Greenwich Avenue.

The Health Pub

371 Second Ave., at East 21st St.
Gramercy Park, Manhattan
529-9200
Open: daily 11 A.M.–11 P.M.
By subway: 6 to 23rd St.
Average price per entree: $8
Alcohol: none
Credit: none
Reservations: none
Classification: Wholesome Hideaway
Pièce de résistance: blue corn enchiladas with anasazi beans and tomatillo sauce

The Health Pub is not for everyone. Some will say it's not for anyone. But people who adhere to, try to adhere to, or think about adhering to a healthier diet will feel good about the meatless, eggless, sugarless, nondairy food prepared there. Why, even I liked it, and you know what my diet's like just by leafing through this book.

Food is perhaps the only really interesting thing to look at in the restaurant, with the exception of the much-too-healthy-looking waitresses, who supposedly give us inspiration to eat better. The two peach-toned dining rooms and six-stool juice bar are modern and clean, yet very plain, like a new restaurant missing some final touches.

The five entrees are each wonders of imaginative cooking, combining scores of vegetable ingredients both common and obscure. Have you tried, for example, quinoa, seitan, anasazi beans, agar, or dandelion, and have you ever had them on a pizza? Well you can read about all this food exotica on the detailed ingredients list that is handed out along with the menu. The best entree is the blue corn enchiladas with anasazi beans and tomatillo sauce, which is much lighter but more flavorful than what we're used to at most Mexican restaurants. Also recommended: whole-grain polenta with sun-dried tomatoes and chick-peas on a bed of greens; steamed mixed vegetables and brown rice with quinoa béchamel; black bean chili with cilantro and tofu sour cream. My one big nay vote goes to the sautéed seitan (wheat gluten) with shiitake mushrooms over ginger mustard greens. Being healthy is only worth so much.

Desserts—hazelnut carob torte, poppyseed cake with lemon sauce, autumn squash pie—look inviting and they might even delight someone who's on a restricted diet, but they just don't excite. I'd rather skip 'em, sip an herbal tea, and dream about pecan pie à la mode.

Hooper's Choice

2221 Boston Rd., near Pelham Pkwy.
The Bronx
881-2424
Open: seven days 7 A.M.–2 A.M.
By subway: 2 to Pelham Pkwy.

Price per burger: $1.99
Alcohol: beer and wine coolers
Credit: none
Reservations: none
Classification: Funky Casual
Pièce de résistance: burger and a milk shake

Where do you take the kids to eat after a trip to the Bronx Zoo or New York Botanical Garden? The choice has gotta be Hooper's, a gleaming-white, fast-food fortress at the junction of Boston Post Road, White Plains Road, and Pelham Parkway. This prototype for a new hamburger chain serves American roadside favorites in a whimsical space that's more fun than Pee-wee Herman's Playhouse. The revolving-door entrance, the glass brick and neon details, the red fiberglass tables, turquoise seats, and shiny black chairs are all slick and cheerful, incorporating pop motifs from the past and visions of the future. The stylized booths resemble gondolas set to zoom through a twenty-first-century, music-video funhouse.

The happiest surprise is the food, which could be considered old-fashioned in a pre–Big Mac sense. Everything is made fresh: crinkle-cut fries, onion loaves, broiled burgers, salads, chicken, fried shrimp, ice cream treats. When done right, the burgers, enhanced by nice sesame buns and a do-it-your-way fixings bar, easily outclass the big chains'; you can even order one that actually looks and tastes medium rare. The crisp-edged, juicy fried chicken is a standout and so's the char-broiled chicken sandwich as a lower-calorie alternative. The deep-dish pizzas are not without merit, but put quite simply, they are not welcome in the Bronx.

Don't leave Hooper's without a malted or milk shake. They are mixed to order with Hooper's own premium ice cream, syrup, milk, and malt to educate a whole generation of kids raised on McDonald's and Burger King's synthetic shakes.

Horn & Hardart Dine-O-Mat

942 Third Ave., near East 57th St.
Midtown Manhattan
755-3755
Open: seven days 7 A.M.–2 A.M.
By subway: N, R to Lexington Ave.; 4, 5, 6 to 59th St.

1 University Pl., near Waverly Pl.
Greenwich Village, Manhattan
254-6160
Open: Sun.–Thurs. 8 A.M.–midnight, Fri. & Sat. till
  2 A.M.
By subway: N, R to 8th St.

Average lunch prices: sandwiches $6.75, entrees $8
Alcohol: yes
Credit: AE, DC, MC, V
Reservations: none
Classification: Funky Casual
Pièce de résistance: boneless breast of country-fried
  chicken

The Dine-O-Mats are much more than just two more trendy retro-diners celebrating the glorified symbols of 1950s Americana. They're also exhilarating look-and-taste tributes to the badly missed Horn & Hardart Automat cafeterias.

Besides the glowing fifties' diner details that make the place bop (speckled laminate counter,

Wurlitzer jukebox, glass-brick trimming, tiled floors, uniformed waitresses in bobby socks), the spiffy Third Avenue Dine-O-Mat is also decorated with two classic Automat fixtures: a set of coin-operated food windows and a coffee station. Along the walls there are black-and-white photographs of the old New York automats. The addition of this memorabilia is an act of courage in itself, since there's no way that any new restaurant can live up to the grandeur of those Art Deco fast-food palaces.

Happily, the Dine-O-Mat often succeeds where it counts most: in the kitchen. Because they're prepared on a much smaller scale, such revived H&H standards as baked beans, creamed spinach, meat loaf, macaroni and cheese, fishcakes, and rice pudding may be better than ever. What's more, what's really more, are the enormous portions. Lunch entrees ($6.95 to $9.95) come with mashed potatoes and gravy, a julienne of steamed veggies, and a Big Apple muffin, which should be mandatory anyway. (Dinner entrees are priced up and out of this guide's range.)

Among the recommended dishes: boneless breast of country-fried chicken with homestyle gravy (the lightly crisp coating is perfect), the hot open meat loaf sandwich with brown gravy, the chicken pot pie (more like a chicken stew with two flaky pastry saucers), and the mountainous side order of macaroni and cheese ($2.50).

Also on the menu are salad platters, sandwiches, burgers, kosher franks, and some most welcome New York soft drinks: egg creams and Dr. Brown's sodas. As for dessert, the proof is in the rice pudding.

The Hourglass Tavern

373 West 46th St., near Ninth Ave.
Theater District, Manhattan
265-2060
Open for lunch: Mon.–Fri. 11:30 A.M.–3 P.M.; open for
    dinner: Mon.–Thurs. & Sun. 5:30 P.M.–10:30 P.M.,
    Fri. & Sat. till 11:30 P.M.
By subway: A, C, E to 42nd St.
Average price per complete dinner: $11.50
Alcohol: yes
Credit: none
Reservations: none
Classification: Positively NYC
Pièce de résistance: plat du jour

If the Hourglass Tavern were a newsstand, there
wouldn't be enough room for the Sunday papers or
king-sized cigarettes. Somehow, they've managed
to squeeze twenty-two seats into this sliver of Restaurant Row, where, in a tiny exposed kitchen, the
chef, elbows always bent, prepares wonderful bargain dinners. The odd interior resembles a cheap
theater set's version of a midwestern tavern's version of a medieval inn.

The "NBC Nightly News" report on the Hourglass Tavern exaggerated ever so slightly the sorry
fate of lingering patrons. The Hourglass does im-
pose a fifty-nine-minute time limit on all diners (an
hourglass hovers over each table to keep time), but
few exceed their allotment or get thrown out on
their ears. You shouldn't mind the restriction since
it keeps prices low and shortens the wait for a table.

For $11.50, guests select an appetizer and a choice of five meat, pasta, poultry, or fish daily entrees. They also get a surprise hors d'oeuvre and a warm miniloaf of potato-water bread (mmm!). The richly seasoned food easily outclasses the low fee and tacky decor. Two examples: pink and tender roast leg of lamb spiced with rosemary and Dijon mustard and served in a red wine sauce or the sautéed blackfish in a sun-dried tomato and red wine sauce. Appetizers are far from throwaways. I once had the pleasure of chilled potato-and-leek soup, enlivened by smoked mozzarella and a nice mixed green salad with tarragon-Dijon vinaigrette.

You should finish your dinner with plenty of time to spare—maybe as much as six or seven minutes—unless of course you're one of those slow-pokes who chews a mouthful of Jell-O thirty-two times. Then I'd urge you to stay away, as would the tavern's timekeeper.

Hwa Yuan

40 East Broadway, near Catherine St.
Chinatown, Manhattan
966-5534
Open: Sun.–Thurs. noon–10 P.M., Fri. & Sat. till 11 P.M.
By subway: 6, J, M, N, R to Canal St.; B, D, Q to
    Grand St.; F to East Broadway

Flushing Hwa Yuan

49-97 Main St., at Maple Ave.
Flushing, Queens
(718) 762-8100

Open: Mon.–Thurs. 11:30 A.M.–10:30 P.M., Fri. & Sat.
till 11 P.M., Sun. till 10 P.M.
By subway: 7 to Main St.

Average price per entree: $6.25
Alcohol: beer at Chinatown location only
Credit: AE, MC, V
Reservations: for large groups
Classification: Ethnic Treasure
Pièce de résistance: cold noodles with sesame sauce

Chinatown is one of the few neighborhoods in
metropolitan New York where Szechuan is not the
dominant Chinese cuisine. Still, Hwa Yuan serves
up that hot and spicy food with a flair worthy of a
special trip. And the new Flushing Hwa Yuan, just
a short trip away from Shea Stadium and the
National Tennis Center, is perfect for a pregame or
post-match dinner.

Hwa Yuan is famous for its cold noodles with
sesame sauce and it's hard to believe that any group
would pass up an order. But I'm also quite attached
to the noodles with hot brown meat sauce (a meal
in itself at $3.95) and the noodles with chili sauce.
As for the vast selection of poultry, seafood, beef,
pork, and vegetable standards, close your eyes,
point to any dish, and you're bound to pick a
winner. If only the racetrack were this easy. Three
standouts: sliced abalone and chicken soup; eggplant with spicy garlic sauce; and in Flushing,
General Chicken (incredibly juicy, crispy, tender
morsels of fried chicken with vegetables).

The recently renovated Chinatown Hwa Yuan
is better-dressed than most of its neighbors, but it's

still a noisy and frantic place to dine. Flushing, on the other hand, is a comfortable room with Art Deco details and cool colors balancing the hot food.

Indian Cafe

2791 Broadway, near West 107th St.
Upper West Side, Manhattan
749-9200
Open: seven days 11:30 A.M.–midnight
By subway: 1 to 110th St.
Alcohol: yes

201 West 95th St., near Broadway
Upper West Side, Manhattan
222-1600
Open: seven days 11:30 A.M.–11:30 P.M.
By subway: 1, 2, 3 to 96th St.
Alcohol: beer and wine

Average price per entree: $7
Credit: AE, MC, V
Reservations: none
Classification: A Little Romance
Pièce de résistance: lamb muglai

Some nights the homelike charm of a no-frills ethnic eatery is insufficient for the mood of the moment. Both Indian Cafes satisfy your taste for spiritedly spiced food with easy touches of romance and elegance. The newer, larger location on Broadway near 107th Street, with its attractive, glass-enclosed sidewalk cafe and full bar, is particularly well-suited for movie-and-dinner dates. (The Olympia Twin Cinemas are situated directly across Broadway.)

Indian Cafe's menu is basic and reliable, the selection satisfying but never eye-popping, even with the addition of a few specials. All food is cooked mild but can be prepared hotter if you so desire. I usually concentrate on the special selections, but they do a particularly nice job with such everyday vegetarian dishes as chick-peas with spinach and tomato, whole baby okra with red bell peppers, and lentils sautéed in ghee (an Indian butter) with ginger and garlic. Among the meat recommendations: lamb muglai or chicken muglai (in a sauce of yogurt and almonds) and goat curry with almonds.

For an appetizer, consider the samosas (deep-fried vegetable-filled pastries), the vegetable or chicken pakoras (fritters), and the three Indian breads: paratha, roti, or poori.

J. West

745 Ninth Ave., near West 50th St.
Clinton, Manhattan
582-2288
Open: Mon.–Thurs. 11:30 A.M.–11 P.M., Fri. & Sat. till midnight
By subway: C, E to 50th St.
Average price per entree: $7.75
Alcohol: yes
Credit: AE, MC, V
Reservations: not necessary
Classification: A Little Romance
Pièce de résistance: crispy orange beef

Jack Dempsey used to sit by the window of his Broadway restaurant all day long to attract customers. Well, the Manassa Mauler wasn't available, so J. West obtained the services of two lifelike mannequins named Frank and Ma to pose in its window. What's doubly odd about these dummy artworks is that they look like grumpy dinner guests. But a gimmick is a gimmick and J. West had to set itself apart from the dozen or so Chinese restaurants that seem to be opening on Ninth Avenue each week.

J. West is an offshoot of J. East, a Flushing eatery with a faithful clientele that is 95 percent Chinese. The new menu, broadened for the Manhattan West crowd, is a spirited melange of Szechuan-, Cantonese-, and Taiwanese-style cooking. What pleases me most about J. West is that the food is prepared and served in a manner that outclasses its price range.

The prawns Szechuan style, for example, are enticingly presented with the bright orange prawns framed on each side by steamed broccoli. They fulfill their promise. The homemade, handmade steamed Shanghai pork dumplings are imprinted with a lovely leaf-like pattern and served in a handsome bamboo steamer.

People who go for sweeter dishes like crispy orange beef and lemon chicken will go wild for them here. Also recommended: crispy trio delight (lightly fried prawns, scallops, and fish fillet with a tomato-based dip made with rice wine, vinegar, and hot red pepper); moo shoo pork; and the baby clams with black bean sauce. Only the curried chicken was a letdown. There are also five low-calorie, low-cholesterol, low-sodium "spa" dishes and incredible $3.95 to $6.95 lunch specials (the crispy orange beef is among them).

Playful crayon drawings made by dinner guests, inspired perhaps by the sesame oil–accented bean curd and vegetable soup, adorn the walls of the tidy, modern dining room.

Jackson Diner

37-03 74th St., near 37th Ave.
Jackson Heights, Queens
(718) 672-1232
Open: daily 11:30 A.M.–10 P.M.
By subway: 7 to 74th St.; E, F, G, R to Roosevelt Ave.
Average price per entree: $6
Alcohol: none
Credit: none
Reservations: none
Classification: Ethnic Treasure
Pièce de résistance: boti kebab

Once in a while Campbell's probably puts the wrong label on a can of soup, say tomato bisque in place of split pea. It happens to restaurants too. The Jackson Diner has the wrong label and the wrong container for its food. But just as thousands of people got used to drinking gin from a coffee mug during prohibition, you too can accept the idea of eating Indian food in a 1950s American diner.

The Jackson Diner is the height of low fashion, a fifties dining car with marbelized Formica walls of the palest blue-green shade and walnut-veneer tables and chairs. The expert Indian cooking, however, is as lively as the diner is plain.

When guests of Indian descent order dinner, the waiter or waitress asks if they'd like their food prepared medium or spicy. Non-Indians get the choice of medium or mild. Don't be insulted. The medium is already sufficiently spicy, so the dual standard is probably in your best interest.

The menu of ten vegetarian and nineteen non-vegetarian entrees is a hit from top to bottom ($4.95 to $6.95). Tandoor mixed grill offers a sampling of their fine, never-overcooked chicken and lamb tandoor specials. The best is boti kebab (succulent pieces of lamb marinated in a special masala sauce). Another fine lamb dish is kadai ghost (lamb chunks in a heavily spiced tomato-based sauce cooked in a kadai, the Indian equivalent of a wok). A sure bet in the vegetarian column: baingan bhuarta (a yummy puree of broiled eggplant cooked with onions, tomatoes, ginger, and chilies).

The dessert most consistent with American tastes is the kulfi (similar to pistachio ice cream), but give the other more exotic desserts a try, especially the rasmalai (cheese balls in milk). Bet you never had this stuff in a diner before.

Jai Ya

81-11 Broadway, near Pettit Pl.
Elmhurst, Queens
(718) 651-1330
Open: seven days noon–midnight
By subway: G, R to Elmhurst Ave.

Average price per entree: $7.25
Alcohol: yes
Credit: AE, MC, V
Reservations: accepted
Classification: Ethnic Treasure
Pièce de résistance: Jai Ya special baked shrimp

Hip chili peppers love to dance at Jai Ya. They go to mingle with ginger, curry, basil, and others in scintillating sauces, prepared "mild hot and spicy," "hot and spicy," or "very hot and spicy." Interpret those grades, respectively, as hot, very hot, and lethal.

Jai Ya is reputedly one of New York's few authentic Thai restaurants. Having never been to Thailand, I cannot confirm this. But I can tell you that this is a sensational restaurant, easily worth a special trip to Queens. The dimly lit, comfortable dining room is an appropriately cool and mysterious setting for the torrid food affairs afforded within.

For piquant starters that two can share, you might try the sweet and spicy nam-sod (ground pork mixed with onion, fresh chili, ginger, peanuts, and lemon juice) or nur-yang-num tok (strips of rare barbecued beef mixed with fresh mint, white onion, ground dried chili, and lemon juice). Each is served at room temperature. In addition, few can resist the spicy shrimp soup, served ceremoniously in a flaming hot pot.

Approach the green chilies ever so carefully when ordering Jai Ya's wonderful pork, beef, chicken, or shrimp dishes with chili and basil leaves ($6.75 to $7.95). I've seen their pictures in the post office. A milder selection that's highly recommended is the Jai Ya special baked shrimp, a clay pot of four snappy, flavorful jumbo shrimp over a bed of glass noodles in ginger sauce.

Exotic Thai ice creams, including such flavors as jasmine-palm and coconut-black bean, are most-welcome desserts. The frosted beer mugs that come with bottles of the Thai beer, Singha, are a god-send.

Jeremy's Ale House

254 Front St., at Dover St.
Financial District, Manhattan
964-3537
Open: Mon.–Fri. 8 A.M.–8:45 P.M., Sat. & Sun. 11 A.M.–
  7 P.M.
By subway: 2, 3, 4, 5, J, M, R to Fulton St.;
  A, C to Broadway-Nassau
Average price per fish 'n' chips plate: $4.25
Alcohol: yes
Credit: none
Reservations: are you kidding?
Classification: Positively NYC
Pièce de résistance: fried calamari and a bucket
  of beer

Anticipating the boom of the South Street Sea-port, Jeremy's pitched its beer taps on Front Street six years ago and evolved from a makeshift, blue-collar seafood tavern into a favorite gathering spot for Wall Street's young professionals. It would be easy to say that this transformation has ruined Jeremy's, but it's simply not true, at least not during off-peak hours (stay away on Fridays after 5 P.M., unless you fancy the idea of being crushed by the yuppie stampede). It's still a great spot to grab some fish 'n' chips and one of Jeremy's notorious buckets of beer. In addition, Jeremy's expansion to this large garage space during the summer of 1988 eased much of the overcrowding.

For fried fish or seafood and chips, I don't know of a better value or a better batter in town than Jeremy's fried-to-order platters ($3.25 to $5.50): fish, scallops, shrimp, or calamari served with a choice of tartar sauce, cocktail sauce, or horseradish. And don't overlook the oversized meat heros, especially the rare roast beef.

Now, back on the subject of beer, be warned that a large draft beer at Jeremy's means a thirty-two-ounce Styrofoam bucket, enough to push light-weights overboard after just one round. I'm not exactly sure how they got so popular, but it's easy to understand why Wall Streeters observing a one-beer limit at lunchtime seem to like them.

Johnny's Reef

2 City Island Ave.
City Island, Bronx
885-2090
Open: Sun.–Thurs. 11 A.M.–midnight, Fri. & Sat. till
    2 A.M. (Closed mid-December until Valentine's Day)
By subway: 2, 5 to Pelham Pkwy. or 6 to Pelham Bay
    Park, then Bx 12 City Island bus to last stop
Average price per seafood platter: $7
Alcohol: yes
Credit: none
Reservations: none
Classification: Positively NYC
Pièce de résistance: fried shrimp

What distinguishes City Island from any quaint, charming, run-of-the-mill New England fishing village is its Bronx accent. Boroughbreds don't go to City Island; they go to (say it in a millisecond) Ciddy-I-lin.

And they go for the bracing pleasures of seaside dining, which might feature a two-pound lobster at one of the Island's many moderate-to-expensive seafood restaurants or a basket of fried shrimp and chips at Johnny's Reef. At the southern end of the island both in location and price, Johnny's wide-open patio boasts a superior view of Long Island Sound and points beyond. The patio is only furnished with ninety powder-blue picnic tables and fishing lines strung overhead to ward off seagulls.

Indoors, Johnny's is a clean, counter-service-only family restaurant and bar with about forty tables. The generously portioned, nongreasy fried-fish selections are mostly $5 to $10 and come with fresh Idaho fries and a cup of cole slaw. The fresh fish is first dunked in an egg-and-butter batter, coated with fine cracker meal, and then deep-fried to order. The good-sized, snappy shrimp is the best catch, though the sea scallops are moist and sweet and the clams are plentiful. Whiting is probably the top value at $6.

As side attractions, the buttered corn on the cob and cleanly fried onion rings ought to be required eating. The Manhattan clam chowder is decent; leave the hot dogs and the gloppy thick shakes for the kiddies.

John's Pizzeria

278 Bleecker St., near Seventh Ave. So.
Greenwich Village, Manhattan
243-1680
Open: Mon.–Sat. 11:30 A.M.–midnight, Sun. noon–
midnight
By subway: 1 to Christopher St.; A, C, E, F to West 4th
St.
Alcohol: beer and wine

408 East 64th St., near First Ave.
Upper East Side, Manhattan
935-2895
Open: Mon.–Sat. 11:30 A.M.–midnight, Sun. noon–
midnight
By subway: 4, 5, 6 to 59th St.; N, R to Lexington Ave.
Alcohol: yes

Average price per large pizza: $9
Credit: none
Reservations: none
Classification: Positively NYC
Pièce de résistance: sausage and mushroom pizza

Nineteen eighty-nine marks the sixtieth anniver-
sary of John's, the legendary Greenwich Village
pizzeria Woody Allen made world-famous. Woody
filmed a scene from *Manhattan* in John's and cast its
current owner, Pete Castellotti, in *Broadway Danny
Rose*, *The Purple Rose of Cairo*, and *Radio Days*. Only
in a pizza-crazy town like New York could a pizza
maestro become a movie star.

A person who can bake a pizza crust like this deserves fame. John's pies are charred dark brown on the edges with burn spots scattered on the bottom, the result of sitting in the superhot, coal-heated brick oven for six minutes (gas-heated pizzas cook for about fifteen minutes). Many first-timers see a John's pizza and complain that it's over-cooked. But one bite of the crispy but not brittle crust and they're sold for life.

John's offers fifty-four combinations of fresh top-pings—from the basic cheese (mozzarella) and to-matoes to cheese, tomatoes, anchovies, sausage, peppers, meatballs, onions, and mushrooms—but nothing trendy like goat cheese, sun-dried toma-toes, or sushi. The cheese-tomatoes-sausage-mushrooms combo is the best seller; cognoscenti demand fresh garlic. My only complaint is that pies are sometimes too sparsely dressed, maybe even a little skimpy. John's also bakes an outstanding calzone: an enormous, half moon–shaped pizza turnover stuffed with ricotta, mozarella, and sau-sage.

After its pizzas, John's is probably best known for the long lines of people waiting outside during peak hours. These have shortened considerably since the expansion of the original store and the opening of the dressier East Side location. Which John's is better? I'm partial to the original with its anti-quated wood booths and tacky murals, but the East Side is saner and more stylish and even has an outdoor patio. Either way, don't sweat it—the pizzas are nearly identical.

Katz's Delicatessen

205 East Houston St., at Ludlow St.
Lower East Side, Manhattan
254-2246
Open: Sun.–Thurs. 7 A.M.–11 P.M., Fri. & Sat. till 1 A.M.
By subway: F to Second Ave.; J, M to Essex St.
Average price per sandwich: $5
Alcohol: beer
Credit: none
Reservations: none
Classification: Positively NYC
Pièce de résistance: corned beef sandwich

CUSTOMER *(TO COUNTERMAN AT KATZ'S DELI)*:
There's a fly on my pastrami sandwich.

COUNTERMAN:
You'll have to give that back then. You didn't order a combination.

They finally took the "No Tipping" signs down from behind the counter at Katz's, the Lower East Side's enduring Jewish-style, nonkosher delicatessen. For years, Katz's regulars have known that if you don't tip the counterman, you're liable to get a pastrami or corned beef sandwich with an inch of questionably brown meat. Slip him fifty cents or a buck, however, and you get twice as much nice-looking pink meat, extra pickles, and a nosh of meat while you wait, a memorable reward for an unspoken understanding.

The most frequent complaint heard at Katz's, or any authentic New York delicatessen for that matter, is that the corned beef and pastrami are too fatty. I must agree with counterman Robert Krinsky when he responds, "If God wanted pastrami to be lean, cows would be lean too." Amen.

Katz's sells five products: pastrami, corned beef (they do their own pickling), franks, garlicky salami, and bologna (which they'll ship all over the world). The L-shaped corner restaurant, as informal (and on Sundays, as busy) as a subway station, is one of the city's largest. The old custom on the Lower East Side of distributing tickets to customers as they enter is still practiced. Countermen mark off prices on the ticket when they take an order. The ticket is later presented to the cashier for payment. Those who lose their tickets are required either to pay the maximum amount or, heaven forbid, clean the premises.

Kuan Sing Dumpling House

9 Pell St., near Bowery
Chinatown, New York
349-0503
Open: seven days 10 A.M.–10 P.M.
By subway: 6, J, M, N, Q, R to Canal St.; B, D, Q to Grand St.; F to East Broadway
Average price per entree: $3.50
Alcohol: none
Credit: none
Reservations: none
Classification: Ethnic Treasure
Pièce de résistance: boiled dumplings with beef and cabbage

I wouldn't call the kitchen at Kuan Sing a steam-bath, but I hear that jockeys and fashion models stop in from time to time to lose weight. All day long the cooks are in there steaming and boiling dumplings for a steady flow of regulars just crazy about those pockets of love.

In most Chinese restaurants, dumplings are enjoyed as appetizers. Here they are rarely the side act. An order of ten plump, boiled dumplings filled with beef and cabbage and delivered in a bamboo steamer will test your chopstick dexterity but never your loyalty. Equally special are their smaller cousins floating around in the wonton soup.

Those who want a little more variety might try a plate of vegetables or a noodle dish. The best of the latter is Kuan Sing fried noodles, a mountain of linguine-like noodles topped with – are you ready – pork, beef, chicken, baby shrimp, mushrooms, broccoli, onions, and scallions, all for $3.95. Rice cooked in Chinese vegetable broth makes a nice lunch at $2.15.

A quick glance at any of Kuan Sing's mirrored walls creates the illusion that there are an endless number of dining rooms, not just the one with a dozen tables. Fortunately, the first glimpse of their dumplings is no mirage.

La Bonne Soupe

48 West 55th St., near Sixth Ave.
Midtown, Manhattan
586-7650
Open: seven days 11:30 A.M.–midnight
By subway: E, F, N, R to Fifth Ave.

Average price per soup special: $6.50
Alcohol: yes
Credit: AE
Reservations: no
Classification: Wholesome Hideaway
Pièce de résistance: soupe à l'oignon

While a square foot of retail space on Fifth Avenue in the mid-50s rents for up to five hundred dollars per month, a seat around the corner at La Bonne Soupe, with glass of wine, basket of French bread, green salad, bowl of soup, and chocolate mousse or crème caramel, goes for $6.50 per visit. Luckily, this is one restaurant that does not totally reflect the character of its neighborhood.

La Bonne Soupe is a cozy midblock bistro with two levels for resting legs and shopping bags and ingesting invigorating bowls of steaming, blue-chip stocks. Their four soupes toujours are soupe à l'oignon (deep-golden French onion soup with crusty cheese clinging to the rim), soupe paysanne a l'orge (hearty mushroom and barley with bits of lamb), crème Andalouse (richly stocked tomato-vegetable), and soupe aux choix à la Russe (sweet-and-sour cabbage). All flourish in the company of the freshly baked, crusty French bread delivered to each table. The soupspoons and butter knives at La Bonne Soupe must feel as spoiled as any utensil in Trump Tower.

Those both pooped out and souped out should opt for one of the four fluffy, moist omelets ($6.75), especially the omelette aux epinards (filled, not speckled, with spinach and sliced mushrooms).

La Caridad

2199 Broadway, at West 78th St.
Upper West Side, Manhattan
874-2780
Open: Mon.–Sat. 11:30 A.M.–midnight, Sun. till
   10:30 P.M.
By subway: 1 to 79th St.
Average price per entree: $4.15
Alcohol: none
Credit: none
Reservations: none
Classification: Ethnic Treasure
Pièce de résistance: roast pork Cuban style

If you think La Caridad is a little scruffy, you should've seen the place ten years ago. At that time, this Chinese-Latino eatery was a grungy corner lunch counter catering to Spanish-speaking taxicab drivers, deliverymen, and a handful of daring student types who couldn't afford to eat anywhere else.

News of good eats, however, travels fast in this town. Pretty soon La Caridad became a West Sider's best excuse not to cook at home. The Cuban-Chinese fare was found to be terrific, the beans and rice were regarded as "eat to win" food, and the rock-bottom prices almost made up for the helium apartment rents in the neighborhood.

The "new" La Caridad, expanded and remodeled to satisfy the increased demand, is more cheerful and colorful than the original. The Cuban and Chinese food, however, is happily the same; the prices still unreal. Such personal favorites as shredded beef (ropa vieja), pepper steak, roast pork. Cuban style, pork chops, chicken crackling, and crispy fried pork, all served with mountains of rice and beans (my preference is black beans and yellow rice), are under $5. And it's good eating, even with the occasional overdose of chopped garlic. The piping-hot Cantonese style dishes are popular, too, though I've mostly ignored that side of the menu.

The best sides are fried sweet banana and avocado salad. And be sure to close with a cafe con leche (espresso with milk).

La Kocina Filipina

69-10 Roosevelt Ave., near 69th St.
Woodside, Queens
(718) 651-0594
Open: daily 10:30 A.M.–10 P.M.
By subway: 7 to 69th St.
Average price per entree: $4.50
Alcohol: none
Credit: none
Reservations: accepted
Classification: Ethnic Treasure
Pièce de résistance: crispy pata

La Kocina Filipina mostly treats homesickness within Woodside's sizeable Filipino community, but outsiders can get a fine introduction to the cuisine of the Philippines and its Chinese, Spanish, and Malaysian influences.

Filipinos have a penchant for pungent flavors—bitter, sour, and salty—that may make certain dishes disagreeable to American tastes. But everyone simply must try the mildly sour chicken adobe (cooked in soy sauce, garlic, and vinegar), the closest thing the diverse Philippines have to a national dish. La Kocina's most popular item, however, is crispy pata, an ultracrispy, fatty plate of fried pork, seasoned with garlic and vinegar. Other suggestions: kare-kare (oxtail stewed with roasted peanuts and vegetables), lampiang sariwa (vegetable egg rolls topped with peanut sauce), bistek tagalog (sautéed beef strips marinated in soy sauce and lemon).

The desserts, like the selections from the organist who plays nightly, tend to be rich and sweet. Brazo mercedes is a log cake of meringue with a filling of egg yolk and condensed milk. Sans rival, the Filipino equivalent of the napoleon, is a layered pastry of almonds and egg whites. And the kids love to sip sago at gulaman, a syrupy tapioca and gelatin drink.

Laila's

440 Seventh Ave., at 15th St.
Park Slope, Brooklyn
(718) 788-0268
Open: Mon.–Thurs. 3 P.M.–10 P.M., Fri. till 11 P.M., Sat. noon–11 P.M., Sun. noon–10 P.M.
By subway: F to 15th St./Prospect Park
Average price per entree: $8
Alcohol: none
Credit: none
Reservations: none
Classification: Ethnic Treasure
Pièce de résistance: ouzy

As good as the Syrian-Lebanese cooking is at Laila's, most people reluctantly surrender to their humongous dinner portions and leave a third or half unfinished. "What's the matter?" teases the waitress. "You didn't like it? Do you want me to wrap it up for you?" Intuitively she knows the answers: "Nothing's the matter." "No-no, I loved it." "Yes, please do!"

If only she could wrap up the whole restaurant and move it to a corner closer to my apartment. Laila's is what an unaffected, Brooklyn-born Middle Eastern bistro should look, feel, and taste like. The homey white shop displays Persian rugs, ceiling fans, and meatless ouzys. Yes, meatless ouzys, scrumptious phyllo pies filled with rice, beans, nuts, raisins, mushrooms, and green pepper.

Not that you should avoid meat. Laila's prepares their meat dishes with considerable care; the fresh-vegetable accompaniment is never lost in nebulous sauces. Two inspiring examples: fassoulia (chunks of lamb, green beans, and fresh tomato in garlic, lemon, and spices) and muldhoum (chopped meat, eggplant, fresh tomato, mushrooms, and green pepper in tomato sauce, baked under mozzarella cheese). Among other meat specialties are moussaka and chicken kebab.

Appetizers are scored for trios, not solos. Three can handle the lemony combo plate of hummus, baba ganouj, falafel, grape leaves, and salad. Remember, if the menu says appetizer "for two," that means two trios or one happy sextet.

Leo's Famous

861 Sixth Ave., near West 30th St.
Herald Square, Manhattan
564-3264
Open: Mon.–Fri. 7 A.M.–5 P.M.

100 West 32nd St., at Sixth Ave.
Herald Square, Manhattan
695-1099
Open: Mon.–Sat. 7 A.M.–9 P.M., Sun. till 6 P.M.

By subway: B, D, F, N, Q, R to 34th St.
Price per frankfurter: $1.50
Alcohol: none
Credit: none
Reservations: none
Classification: Positively NYC
Pièce de résistance: tube steaks

To most of us, they're just condiments: relish, chili, sauerkraut, onions, the works. To Leo Cohen, frankfurter maven of Sixth Avenue, they're "subterfuge."

"To really appreciate a hot dog," advises Cohen, "you put nothing on it. You see in these shopping malls, they put cheese and bacon on 'em. There's no need for it if it's a good product."

He should know. The franks at Leo's Famous are the best in Manhattan, the way franks used to be. They're beefy, kosher, Hebrew National hot dogs with a natural casing that makes them snap when you bite into them, not like the limp, skinless dogs you buy for fifty cents around town. Spread on a ribbon of deli mustard, enjoy a tonic orange drink, and feel like a top dog.

Leo's two counters are a block-and-a-half apart, so I suggest you go to the one at 861 Sixth where the owner works the grill. Nobody babies a frank like Leo.

"How do you like my beautiful steaks?" Cohen asks a customer. "They're like babies, you can't leave 'em out of your sight."

When a frank is ready — an undercooked one will not snap; an overcookd one will snap on the grill and not in your mouth — there must be someone to buy it. There is an art to timing the movement of franks across the grill so every customer gets one that's properly cooked. It's the difference between a good hot dog and a great tube steak.

"You gotta have that touch," says Cohen.

LeRoy's Coffee Shop

247 West Broadway, near Walker St.
TriBeCa, Manhattan
966-3370
Open: Mon.–Sat. 7 A.M.–5 P.M.
By subway: 1 to Franklin St.; A, C, E to Canal St.
Average price per lunch special: $5
Alcohol: none
Credit: none
Reservations: none
Classification: Positively NYC
Pièce de résistance: eggplant latkes parmigiana

You can walk from West Broadway to Sixth Avenue without leaving LeRoy's, a floor-through wonder of a coffee shop in Manhattan's TriBeCa neighborhood. Situated two-and-a-half blocks south of Canal Street, LeRoy's had welcome mats on two avenues to greet the exodus of artists priced out of SoHo in the late seventies. They were lured by an imaginative extension of the typical coffee shop menu.

Instead of falling into the gentrification trap that's resulted in an abundance of sushi, pasta, and croissant parlors, owner Herb David kept the burgers, BLTs, grilled cheeses, and other greasy-spoon faves — all are dependable choices — and added an original repertoire of wholesome lunch concoctions. Some have been failures; most will shock you out of those cheeseburger blues. A fine example is the Mexican omelet ($4.95) served with batter-fried avocado, medium-hot tomato sauce, crisp home fries, and sourdough spicy herb toast. Incredible! For $4.75, how can you possibly beat the Fiorello La Guardia special, eggplant latkes parmigiana, a Jewish-Italian hybrid possible only in New York. The lightly fried latkes (pancakes) are served with brown rice and fresh zucchini smothered in tomatoes and onions.

Other recommended specials: braised beef and macaroni, vegetable lasagna, chicken croquettes in cheese sauce, and pepper steak with Chinese noodles, brown rice, and Mandarin orange salad with sesame dressing. All are within the $4 to $6 price range. Less unique but just as impressive is the chicken salad sandwich, served open style on sourdough fruit-and-nut bread and topped with a heap of fresh fruit. It's a Joe E. Brown mouthful.

Les Poulets

27 East 21st St., near Broadway
Flatiron District, Manhattan
254-5330
Open: Mon.–Fri. 7:30 A.M.–9:30 P.M., Sat. & Sun.
  noon–8 P.M.
By subway: 6, R, N to 23rd St.
Average price per chicken platter: $4.95
Alcohol: none
Credit: AE, DC
Reservations: none
Classification: Wholesome Hideaway
Pièce de résistance: grilled chicken

Grilled chicken is a fast-growing fast-food com-
modity all over town, but most of its practitioners
are takeout shops providing few amenities for
dining on the premises. A notable exception is Les
Poulets, a cool, clean, modern restaurant serving
some of the finest food you're likely to eat from a
disposable plate.

The cafeteria-style operation features well-
marinated chicken grilled over a gas-heated flame
and served with a choice of five dipping sauces:
American (barbecue), Latin (salsa), French (Dijon),
Japanese (teriyaki), and "clerveau" (garlic). A
combo platter with a half-chicken, cottage fries or
rice (neither excites), and crunchy, vinegary cole
slaw is $4.95. A nice alternative is the homemade
chicken pot pie, which is zestier than what we're
used to, though I don't believe the microwave
reheat does justice to the flaky crust.

One thing still confuses me about this place:
Who is this guy Les Poulets anyway and where did
he go to high school?

Lupe's East L.A. Kitchen

110 6th Ave., at Watts St.
SoHo, Manhattan
966-1326
Open: Sun.–Thurs. 11:30 A.M.–11 P.M., Fri. & Sat. till
  midnight, Sat. & Sun. brunch 11 A.M.–4 P.M.
By subway: E, C to Spring St.; A to Canal St.
Average price per entree: $7
Alcohol: beer
Credit: none
Reservations: none
Classification: Funky Casual
Pièce de résistance: enchiladas mole

The relative obscurity of Lupe's only enhances its aim to duplicate the feel and tastes of an East L.A. eatery. Because it is situated on a SoHo corner with few passersby, diners feel like they're in on something only a handful of locals know about. You're lucky I can't keep a good secret.

The shop has the earthy, unsophisticated look of a barrio hangout, seating forty-two at scattered booths, tables, and a six-stool counter. For art-work, old record jackets featuring cha-cha, merengue, and tango music line the walls. Latin American music fills the room at low volume.

The Mexican standards—burritos, enchiladas, tacos—are praiseworthy for three distinctive home-made chili sauces—red, green (with tomatillos), or mole—each stolen, more or less, from popular dives in East L.A. There is nothing dishonorable or un–New York about this act. Only an insanely chauvinistic New Yorker could make the claim that New York has better Mexican restaurants than Los Angeles. The problem is you can't get to any of theirs by subway.

The superb chiles rellenos (fried peppers stuffed with cheese) are topped with the green chili sauce on one side, the red chili sauce on the other. I can't decide which mood of sauce I like better, but boy do I love trying. Highest grades, however, go to the beef burrito Colorado (stuffed with beans, cheese, and the tastiest beef I've ever had in a burrito) and enchiladas mole, stuffed with chicken and topped with a twenty-ingredient mole sauce which includes various chilies, bitter chocolate, peanuts, and sesame seeds. Less successful are the rather plain taquitos (fried tortilla rolls) and the super vegetarian burrito, an overstuffed powerhouse of beans, guacamole, cheese, tomatoes, and sour cream. All plates are about $7 at dinner; $5 for the same-sized portions at lunch.

Consider also the joys of freshly fried tortilla chips served warm with salsa and the smooth, yummy pumpkin flan, a dessert that will throw you for a Lupe.

Mandarin Court

61 Mott St., near Bayard St.
Chinatown, Manhattan
608-3838
Open: seven days 7 A.M.–11:30 P.M.
By subway: 6, J, M, N, Q, R to Canal St.; B, D, Q to Grand St.
Average price per dim sum lunch: $6.40; per dinner entree: $8
Alcohol: beer

Credit: AE
Reservations: none
Classification: Ethnic Treasure
Pièce de résistance: dim sum

The Chinese residents and habitues of China-town are not loyal to restaurants. They're loyal to chefs. And so if they read in the Chinese papers or hear on the streets that a certain favorite chef is moving to another restaurant, they're likely to follow him. This game of musical woks makes it difficult for outsiders to keep up with the ins and outs of Chinatown.

Opened in mid-April 1988, Mandarin Court became an instant sensation when it was an-nounced in the Chinese papers that dim sum chef Andy Lui had been hired away from Silver Palace, an immense and immensely popular restaurant on the Bowery. Hounding the hoopla led me to Man-darin Court and a better understanding of where I should be on Saturday or Sunday mornings at about 11 A.M.

For the uninitiated, dim sum is an à la carte orgy of fried, steamed, stuffed, stewed, wrapped, or rolled morsels served from carts that are wheeled from table to table. When you select an item from a cart at Mandarin Court, a red star (equal to $1.30) or a circle ($2.50) is marked on your check. Four people dining together might say that Mandarin Court is the world's only twenty-star restaurant.

My preferences have more to do with personal taste than slight variations in quality. Chef Lui's reputation for dim sum artistry is well-earned. I would suggest, however, you not pass up the steamed shrimp roll; the steamed dumplings with shrimp, vegetable, and pork; the sticky, chewy sweet-and-sour pork bowl; the turnip cake with Chinese sausage; the sesame roll; or the egg custard, a delicious tart I'd liken to a poached egg and custard in a pastry shell. Wow! Dim sum is served daily from 7 A.M. to 3 P.M., though it is best to arrive before noon for the freshest and widest selection.

For dinner, Mandarin Court has employed William Wing Hui Wong, former chef at the once-acclaimed Nice restaurant on East Broadway. His specialty is seafood, and I flipped for his sizzling shelled prawns in black bean sauce. The commendable braised duck with sea cucumber and Chinese mushrooms is not for everyone; the less-exotic barbecued tenderloin skewers in black pepper sauce are.

Mandarin Court, with its subtly modern decor of plum walls and black tables and chairs, is poised for a long and successful run on Mott Street—if they can ink Lui and Wong to long-term contracts.

Manganaro's Hero-Boy

492 Ninth Ave., near West 37th St.
Clinton, Manhattan
947-7325
Open: Mon.–Sat. 6:30 A.M.–8 P.M.
By subway: A, C, E to 34th St.
Average price per hero: $4
Alcohol: beer and wine
Credit: none
Reservations: none
Classification: Positively NYC
Pièce de résistance: mile-high special

According to Hero-Boy partners Jimmy and Mario Dell'Orto, the hero got its name at their sandwich shop some forty years ago. As legend would have it, Clementine Paddleford, a food scribe for the now-defunct New York *Herald-Tribune*, took a few bites from one of Dell'Orto's heavy handfuls and remarked: "You have to be a hero to finish one of these!"

There is much truth to the observation, if not the story. Hero-Boy is famous for its six-foot heros, but even the individual ones pack a punch. Heavyweights can easily lose a TKO to the mile-high special: prosciutto, salami, mortadella, capicolla, cooked salami, provolone, roasted peppers, tomato, and lettuce. What a sandwich! I get full just writing about it. Other varieties in the same weight class include veal parmigiana; peppers and eggs; salami, provolone, and peppers; prosciutto, mozzarella, and tomato; and on Wednesdays and Fridays, melted mozzarella and eggs. Heros, made on fresh, crusty Italian white or seeded semolina bread, are $2.75 to $5.95.

Of course a tall-neck beer or two goes beautifully with any of the heros, but it sure won't help you go the distance.

Hero-Boy is a ten-minute walk from both the Port Authority and Madison Square Garden. (Most people need a long walk after eating there anyway.) The friendly shop is colored like the Italian flag—red, white, and green—with plenty of space for the sandwiches and the heroic eaters who take them on.

Manhattan Chili Co.

302 Bleecker St., near Seventh Ave.
Greenwich Village, Manhattan
206-7163
Open: seven days noon–midnight
By subway: 1 to Christopher St.; A, B, C, D, E, F, Q to
    West 4th St.
Average price per chili: $7.95
Alcohol: yes
Credit: AE, MC, V
Reservations: for parties of five or more
Classification: Funky Casual
Pièce de résistance: Texas Chain Gang chili

No, Manhattan Chili Co. is not a Fortune-500 company. But it is one of the hotter entrees on the "Under $15 100" and a leading employer of jalapeño peppers. Manhattan Chili Co. manufactures six premium chilies, from the mild Abilene Choral Society chili (ground beef, beans, tomato, white wine, and basil) to the hot-but-not-deadly Texas Chain Gang chili (a soupy blend of ground and diced beef, jalapeños, tomatoes, and beans), first-prize winner in the 1986 New York State Chili Cookoff. Each chili is served with one or more of the following: sour cream, red onion, white onion, diced tomato, cilantro, mixed cheese. Fabulous, crunchy cole slaw also comes in the package.

The lumpy guacamole dip, accented with cilantro and red onion, may be the best I've ever had. Two to four people can easily share a $5 order of dip and chips. Most other appetizers and southwestern entrees will push you over the $15 barrier, as will a couple of rounds of hard-to-resist, fresh-lime frozen margaritas.

Manhattan Chili Co.'s desert decor is pleasantly understated: clay-colored tiled floor, matching brick and salmon-colored walls, slatted oak chairs. Its primary atmospheric asset, however, is the cozy backyard garden, which transforms this chili producer into a summertime oasis hidden from the bustle but not the magic of the Village.

Marti Kebab

228 East 24th St., near Second Ave.
Gramercy Park, Manhattan
545-0602
Open: seven days 11:30 A.M.–11:30 P.M.
By subway: 6 to 23rd St.
Average price per entree: $8.25
Alcohol: none
Credit: none
Reservations: none
Classification: Ethnic Treasure
Pièce de résistance: Iskender kebab

Mediterranean flavors more familiar to us in Greek and Middle Eastern cooking are orchestrated with culinary skill and familial love at Marti Kebab, a precious Turkish cafe and grill hidden on East 24th St. Though just a dot on the Manhattan map, this plain, wood-paneled, seven-table eatery is a gold star on the trail of ethnic treasures.

The appetizer list entices with such regional favorites as hummus, spinach pie, stuffed grape leaves, and falafel, but be sure at least one person at your table tries tarama and imam bayildi. Tarama is a puree of red caviar and olive oil comparable to the Greek delicacy taramosalata. At Marti Kebab it is light, fluffy, and irresistable as a pita bread spread. Imam bayildi (translation: the priest fainted) is eggplant stuffed and smothered with tomatoes, onions, and green pepper granish — a meal in itself for $3.50.

Seven of the ten entrees are kebabs. You can order a mixed grill and try an assortment on one plate, or zero in on three of the best: kofte kebab, char-grilled ground lamb and beef patties, pink and juicy inside and amply seasoned with herbs and spices; iskender kebab, juicy doner meat sliced off the rotisserie and served over hot yogurt and under fresh tomato sauce; chicken kebab, char-grilled, marinated cutlet.

For dessert, the pick is sulac, the smoothest, creamiest rice pudding I've ever met, with a Turkish coffee.

Mary Ann's

116 Eighth Ave., at 16th St.
Chelsea, Manhattan
633-0877
Open: seven days noon–11 P.M.
By subway: A, C, E to 14th St.
Average price per entree: $7
Alcohol: yes
Credit: none
Reservations: none
Classification: Positively NYC
Pièce de résistance: pollo Yucatan

On any given night Mary Ann's is so crowded there's barely enough room for the space between Mary and Ann's. People cram their bodies and bellies in there because the Mexican food is darn good, the prices are low, and everything and everyone swings naturally to a NYC beat.

The menu is extensive and reliable, from burritos and enchiladas to special meat and seafood entrees. Pollo Yucatan (only $7.95) is a stirring version of the latter: large, tender, juicy chunks of chicken breast sautéed with scallions, garlic, mushrooms, and red chilis in cheddar cheese sauce. The Aztec ($6.95) is typical of the "above and beyond" triple combo plates: green chicken enchilada, cheese chile relleno (stuffed pepper), soft taco with guacamole, plus refried beans and rice. Almost all choices are attractively displayed and served steaming hot.

I'm much less enthusiastic about the salad plates ($5.95 to $7.95). I'd toss 'em. Take note that lunch at Mary Ann's is one of the best bargains in town. Even better, you might get a little more breathing space.

Moisha's Luncheonette

239 Grand St., at Bowery
Lower East Side, Manhattan
226-0780
Open: seven days 5 A.M.–5 P.M.
By subway: B, D, Q to Grand St.
Average price per lunch item: $6
Alcohol: none
Credit: none

Reservations: none
Classification: Positively NYC
Pièce de résistance: egg cream and French fries

When Moisha and son went into business over forty years ago, trusty corner luncheonettes with a Jewish accent were as much a part of the New York scene as a two-cents plain. Now theirs is a relic to relish, although passersby often pass it by, dissuaded perhaps by the winos who come in from the Bowery. Still, enough people know about Moisha's exhilarating sodas—namely egg creams and lime rickeys (made here with sweet cherry Coke and lime)—to keep the place busy. And now that Dave's Luncheonette (Canal and Broadway) has closed, Moisha is the egg cream king of downtown Manhattan.

Catty-cornered to the old Bowery Savings Bank, Moisha's also serves decent deli sandwiches—say, a Reuben, chopped liver, or brisket—that can be enjoyed with some of the best crinkle-cut French fries around (a playoff with Nathan's would go seven). Omelets, like the one with lox and onions, are reliable, as are the daily meat and dairy specials. Potato latkes (pancakes), a house specialty served with applesauce or sour cream, is the right idea for anyone who can either pass up the fries or doesn't believe that eating potatoes with potatoes is redundant.

Though a scene from the Paul Mazursky film *Moscow on the Hudson* was filmed on the premises, Moisha's interior is unremarkable. But just sitting down at one of the two U-shaped counters and ordering an egg cream, a lime rickey, or maybe a cup of rice pudding is something kind of special.

Moondance Diner

80 Sixth Ave., at Grand St.
SoHo, Manhattan
226-1191
Open: Mon.–Thurs. 8:30 A.M.–11:30 P.M., Fri. & Sat. 24
  hours
By subway: 1, A, C, E to Canal St.
Average price per sandwich: $7
Alcohol: beer and wine
Credit: none
Reservations: none
Classification: Funky Casual
Pièce de résistance: turkey club

The yellow half-moon that revolves atop the
Moondance Diner is a beacon for companions
wandering through a SoHo night. Blue and silver
letters glitter in the wind, beckoning the after-
hours crowd to come inside and share the night's
magic. The door opens and the music plays. "It's a
marvelous night for a moondance . . ."

Though the Moondance is not much more than
a truckstop in dressy clothes—they sell ham 'n' eggs
and champagne by the glass—the place has the
right come-as-you-are feel for a downtown hangout. The dining car's narrow interior, with its long
counter and ten tables-for-four along the windows,
is cozy yet upbeat. And there's also the option of
moonlight dining on the rear patio during warm-
weather months.

Prices are too high. Having said that, let me
recommend the grilled sandwiches on garlic
challah bread. I know it sounds weird (and they are
a little too bready) but they work. I'd go for the

mozzarella, basil, and tomato; the grilled cheese and bacon; or the turkey club anytime. These go great with Moondance's golden, crunchy, home-made onion rings. A large plate, easily enough for three or four to share, is . . . swallow hard . . . $4.95.

Salads like the chicken salad with apples and walnuts (romaine and watercress topped with chicken salad, sliced apples, chopped walnuts, to-matoes, carrots, and scallions; $7.95) are impres-sive; burgers are skippable. For breakfast, the apple pancakes are tempting but the eggs-potatoes-toast-coffee special is a much better deal.

Nathan's Famous

Surf and Stillwell Aves.
Coney Island, Brooklyn
(718) 946-2202
Open: Sun.–Thurs. 8 A.M.–2 A.M., Fri. & Sat. till 4 A.M.
By subway: B, D, F, N to Stillwell Ave./Coney Island
Price per frankfurter: $1.60
Alcohol: beer
Credit: none
Reservations: none
Classification: Positively NYC
Pièce de résistance: frankfurter on a bun

The sentimental strollers along the boardwalk of Coney Island all have the same daydream. They close their eyes for a moment, then reopen them to the sights of the world's playground in its heyday. Suddenly, all the vanished restaurants, arcades, and rides are back. A kid from Borough Park flips his last nickel in the air. If it lands heads, he uses it to buy a subway token; tails, he grabs a frank at Nathan's and walks home.

Coney is now seedy and rundown and a frank is up to $1.60, but don't let that keep you away. The stand opened by Nathan Handwerker in 1916 endures as New York's quintessential fast-food emporium. Nothing short of a happy ending to *Hamlet* could match the thrill from the first explosive bite of a Nathan's frank. In fact, the traditionalists who claim the franks are better at the original store than the newer locales are not romantic fools. The luscious meat and spices are the same, but some franchises forgo the expense of a natural casing. The so-called skinless franks lack that marvelous snap. Of course, the ocean breeze that whistles down from the boardwalk and the classic neon signs above the landmark are factors you can't duplicate.

Nathan's franks do get lonely without a side order of those crisp-edged, golden brown, crinkle-cut, half-moon French fries. The dry Maine potatoes, fried in corn oil, are always hot and fresh, never soggy. What's more, the counterpersons make a habit of overloading each tray of fries.

Other choices at Nathan's rate below the franks and fries, though the fresh, buttered corn on the cob and the fried clams on a bun with tartar sauce are both recommended. The deep-fried soft-shell crabs are juicy and flavorful, but the low-grade crabs have already hardened a bit and the crisp shell splinters in your mouth.

It should be noted that proposals for the revitalization of Coney Island include the construction of a minor league baseball stadium. If the plan is ever implemented, Murray Handwerker, Nathan's son, plans to bid on the contract to sell franks. Nathan's franks at a ball game in Coney Island? Boy, that's something new to dream about on the boardwalk.

New Wave Coffee Shop

937 Madison Ave., near 74th St.
Upper East Side, Manhattan
734-2467
Open: Mon.–Fri. 6 A.M.–9 P.M., Sat. & Sun. till 6 P.M.
By subway: 6 to 77th St.
Average price per sandwich: $3
Alcohol: none
Credit: none
Reservations: none
Classification: Positively NYC
Pièce de résistance: roast turkey sandwich

The New Wave is one of those only-in-New York phenomenons, a trusty though otherwise routine coffee shop frequented by big-time celebs. It's hidden on a posh Madison Avenue block next to the Whitney Museum, down a block from the Carlyle Hotel.

Dustin Hoffman, who discovered the New Wave while filming *Kramer vs. Kramer*, comes in for a well-done, almost-burned buttered roll. Mary Tyler Moore likes a chicken salad sandwich on pita bread. Tony Randall goes for a Swiss cheese on rye. Roy Scheider takes a well-done toasted corn. Michael Nouri has a fresh turkey sandwich. Tony Bennett orders any type of eggs. I prefer the turkey or a grilled cheese, but anything good enough for Bennett is good enough for me. Of course even stars can be fickle. Jessica Lange and Sam Shepard were recently seen coming out of Three Guys, a New Wave competitor up the block.

Still, it'd be hard to match New Wave's attention to little things that matter: chopped green pepper and tomato in the home fries, a shot glass of fresh-squeezed OJ with breakfast, not more than a couple of ice cubes in a soft drink, waiters who never pass up an opportunity to flirt.

But don't go to the New Wave with the sole intention of meeting somebody famous. Just as water won't boil while you're watching the kettle, you can't see the stars with your head in the clouds.

Omonia Cafe

32-20 Broadway, at 33rd St.
Astoria, Queens
(718) 274-6650
Open: Sun.–Thurs. 8 A.M.–2 A.M., Fri. & Sat. till 3 A.M.
By subway: N to Broadway (Queens)
Average price per pastry: $2
Alcohol: liqueurs
Credit: none
Reservations: none
Classification: A Little Romance
Pièce de résistance: ekmek kataifi

Omonia Cafe is an embarrassment of riches, offering forty-five different pastries, twenty-five different cookies, and eighteen different coffees. Still, I go to people-watch. Omonia is the meeting place of the neighborhood. Older men, sipping espressos their doctors forbid, argue about politics. Teenage girls gossip about boys. Estranged companions try to reconcile. It's a beautiful scene, sweetened by the precious pastries and the charm of Astoria, Queens.

Now I wouldn't dare tell you which pastry to order, but I will tease you by describing a few: glazed chocolate layer cake, a chocaholic's dream made with chocolate glaze, sprinkles, cream, and cake; ice cream flambé, any flavor ice cream topped with meringue and set aflame; ekmek kataifi, a layered pastry of kataifi (shredded wheat soaked in syrup), vanilla custard, and whipped cream topped with sliced almonds; baklava, the standard Greek pastry filled with walnuts and almonds. Topping the list of exotic coffees is Omonia's special cafe, made with Midori liqueur, chocolate fudge, and whipped cream.

There's also a nice selection of dessert appetizers or anytime snacks ($7 or less): spinach pie, quiche, pasta, pizza, etc. I suggest saganaki, the Greek grilled cheese (kaseri cheese, dipped in egg and bread crumbs, then deep fried) or the "French toast," which is actually more like a croque monsieur (a ham-and-feta-cheese sandwich dipped in egg and deep fried).

A glass-enclosed sidewalk cafe, Omonia's Euro-glitzy interior is trimmed in green neon and filled with inviting cappuccino-colored tables and chairs on split levels. Just don't forget to study the pastry cases before sitting down.

Once Upon a Sundae

7702 Third Ave., near 77th St.
Bay Ridge, Brooklyn
(718) 748-3412
Open: summer hours, Sun.–Thurs. 8 A.M.–11 P.M., Fri. &
   Sat. till midnight; other times, seven days 8 A.M.–
   9:30 P.M.
By subway: R to 77th St.
Average price per sundae: $2.70
Alcohol: none
Credit: none
Reservations: none
Classification: Positively NYC
Pièce de résistance: super special sundae

With scoop-shop franchises dominating the ice
cream business in New York, it's especially heart-
warming and spine-tingling to be taken to a precious, old-fashioned ice cream parlor like Once
Upon a Sundae. Opened in 1979 as the number of
parlors in the area dwindled, OUAS rescued fixtures from a Fulton Street parlor built around the
turn of the century. The new shop, with its ornate
mahogany woodwork and antique lights, suggests
the elegance of a Victorian cafe.

More significantly, the parlor is owned and operated by the Logue family, the butterfat kings of
Brooklyn. The Logues make their rich and creamy
premium ice creams with a high butterfat content,
a low overrun (the longer you freeze ice cream, the
greater the overrun or expansion from air), and the
finest-quality flavorings.

Raise a spoon to their sweet successes by being gutsy and demanding the super special sundae ($5): three scoops of ice cream, banana, hot fudge, marshmallow, walnuts, fresh whipped cream, sprinkles, and a cherry. If guilt, however, is not your cup of sugar, you might have a regular-sized sundae, a sixteen-ounce ice cream soda, or a dish of ice cream — maybe butter pecan, chocolate chip, or, during the summer, peachy peach.

Once Upon a Sundae also prepares waffles, burgers, sandwiches, and other foods. Several better dining alternatives can be found along Bay Ridge's Third Avenue. "Under $15ers" should try Lento's (70-03 Third Avenue) for the crispiest pizzas ever to come out of an oven.

Oyshe

199 Columbus Ave., at 69th St.
873-3350
Upper West Side, Manhattan
Open: seven days noon–11 P.M.
By subway: 1 to 66th St.
Average price per entree: $8
Alcohol: yes
Credit: AE, DC, MC, V
Reservations: none
Classification: A Little Romance
Pièce de résistance: okonomi-yaki

The Under $15 restaurantgoer window-shops but rarely dines on fashion-conscious Columbus Avenue. Although this is no great loss, it's nice, for a change, to be on the inside looking out, especially if the inside happens to be the Japanese restaurant Oyshe.

Oyshe's split-level, post–high tech interior is as attractively stylish as any storefront on the Columbus strip, yet prices are quite reasonable. You feel like you're paying the chef—not the landlord, the interior decorator, and the maitre d's tailor.

The house specialty is okonomi-yaki, a Japanese-style pancake filled with vegetables, chicken, pork, beef, or seafood and topped with dried seaweed, bonito (flakes of shaved dry fish) and tonkatsu sauce, a rich, sweet-and-pungent sauce which tends to overpower the flavor of the extras. The chopped-vegetable batter for the pancakes looks a lot like cole slaw and maintains its varied texture through cooking on the open grill. The chunky yet light okonomi-yakis, about seven inches in diameter and three-quarters of an inch high, are priced from $6.95 to $10.95.

Oyshe also does a fine job with its five variations of yakisoba (sautéed noodles). The Sapporo (fresh veggies) is $4.95; the Hiroshima (seafood), $8.95. This place exists, however, to showcase okonomi-yaki, which, though no serious threat to the trade deficit, is well worth trying. So are age dofu (lightly fried tofu appetizer) and the $4.95 to $5.95 lunch specials.

By the way, *oyshe* means delicious and sounds much better when said with a Japanese rather than a Yiddish accent.

P. J. Horgan's

42-17 Queens Blvd., near 42nd St.
Sunnyside, Queens
(718) 729-9584
Open: Mon.–Sat. 11:30 A.M.–3 A.M., Sun. noon–3 A.M.
By subway: 7 to 40th St./Lowery St.
Average price per entree: $5
Alcohol: yes
Credit: none
Reservations: none
Classification: Positively NYC
Pièce de résistance: Horgan burger platter

P. J. Horgan's almost qualified for the "A Little Romance" classification. This cherished neighborhood Irish pub may not be the ideal sort of place to take your sweetheart on Valentine's Day, but it's decidedly the right spot for an informal and economical rendezvous between buddies of the opposite sex. Tiffany lamps hang over cozy dark-wood booths where a basket of fresh Irish soda bread is delivered to your table seconds after you sit down. Add a coupla frosted mugs of beer and you're all set.

The hefty Horgan burger or cheeseburger platter is the top choice on the reliable pub menu. Fried seafood plates, especially sweet and tender scallops, are terrific too. The rest of the selections (shepherd's pie, sliced steak, etc.) and daily specials (shrimp scampi, Irish stew, etc.) are predictable in the best sense of the word. No desserts, but the pure Irish coffee with fresh whipped cream is happily understated.

Patisserie Lanciani

177 Prince St., near Sullivan St.
SoHo, Manhattan
477-2788
Open: Tues.-Sat. 8 A.M.-midnight, Sun. 9 A.M.-9 P.M.
By subway: C, E to Spring St.
Average price per pastry, cake, or torte: $5
Alcohol: yes
Credit: AE, MC, V
Reservations: not necessary
Classification: A Little Romance
Pièce de résistance: Grand Marnier cake

Imagine desserts and breakfasts so lyrical they live up the name—say it soft and slow—*Patisserie Lanciani*. The menu at this lovely French pastry shop/cafe lists one affordable fantasy after another: forty-two pastries, cakes, tortes, and puddings; a half-dozen of the finest breakfasts. Five dollars for a pastry, $3 for a cappuccino, and $4.50 for croissant and eggs is pricey, but consider that the crème de la crème is rarely within a $15 budget.

Let me just list a couple of desserts for you: gateau Charlene (chocolate cake with fresh strawberry filling and ganache icing), mousse aux framboises (fresh raspberries, crème fraiche, and cream), dacquoise (layers of hazelnut meringue and butter cream), sacher torte (chocolate almond torte with rum, apricot jam, chocolate fondant icing). Have I seduced you yet?

Breakfast, served weekdays till 2 P.M., weekends till 4 P.M., is Patisserie Lanciani's forte. The scrambled eggs with smoked salmon and onions or salmon roe and crème fraiche ($6.50 each) are dreamy choices and the brioche French toast is splendid if you ask them to soak it well in its egg batter.

Lunch and dinner selections, actually dessert preludes, are reasonably priced, from soup-and-sandwich combinations ($6.50 to $7.95) to meat and pasta entrees ($7 to $12), but you obviously can't do it all for under $15.

The black-and-gray-toned, Art Deco room looks as though it was designed by Busby Berkeley, with a parade of corrugated fiberglass ceiling ornaments framing your grand entrance to and high-kicking exit from the cafe.

Patsy's Pizzeria

2287 First Ave., at 117th St.
East Harlem, Manhattan
534-9783
Open: Tues.–Sun. noon–4 A.M.
By subway: 6 to 116th St. (take a car or taxi if possible)
Average price per pizza: $10
Alcohol: yes
Credit: none
Reservations: none
Classification: Positively NYC
Pièce de résistance: sausage pizza

In 1933 baker Pasquale "Patsy" Lancieri left Marconi's Pastry Shop in the then Italian section of East Harlem to open Patsy's Pizzeria. By the war years, Patsy's was the pizza mecca of New York, a family restaurant by day, an after-hours hangout by night. Showgirls from Harlem nightclubs, waiters from downtown restaurants, and all types of nabobs and nobodies congregated for two basic, classic pies: mozzarella and tomato or bianca (with ricotta cheese and olive oil).

Despite the steady decline of the neighborhood and the business, Patsy's coal oven is still burning. Lancieri's widow, Carmella, says the pies ain't what they used to be, which only makes me want to leap into the nearest time machine. Today Patsy's turns out beautiful, crisp, thin-crusted pies topped with the very best hot sausage. Positively delish!

Patsy's is a clean and pleasant place to dine in a decidedly unpleasant neighborhood. Business is consequently slow, but as a vestige of its heyday, adventurous celebs pop in from time to time: Rodney Dangerfield, Bill Murray, Linda Ronstadt, Jason Robards, Faye Dunaway. Long-time devotee Frank Sinatra once had fifty pies shipped air express to Palm Springs, California.

Primorski

282B Brighton Beach Ave., near Brighton 3rd St.
Brighton Beach, Brooklyn
(718) 891-3111
Open: seven days 11 A.M.–midnight (or later)
By subway: D to Brighton Beach
Average price per entree: $6
Alcohol: yes
Credit: none
Reservations: yes
Classification: Ethnic Treasure
Pièce de résistance: shashlik chalakhashi

Everything we love and hate about wedding receptions—with the possible exception of the in-laws—is found nightly at Primorski, a Brighton Beach ballroom for Russian-style celebrations of life. You haven't lived until you've downed the last vodka and danced the last tango at Primorski.

The happiest surprise is that Primorski's Georgian-Jewish menu falls comfortably into the "Under $15" class. The indisputable pièce de résist-ance, shashlik chalakhashi—incredibly tender and flavorful ribs of lamb grilled on a skewer (more like a saber than a skewer)—is just $7. The other shashlik selections (grilled chicken, sturgeon, pork) are less. A plate of juicy, tender, garlicky chicken kiev stuffed with mushrooms and served with fried potato wedges and cole slaw is $4.95. With prices like these, who needs an excuse to celebrate.

Most of the food fun, however, comes at soup and appetizer time with one great taste after an-other: assorted smoked fish (sable, salmon, stur-geon, swordfish), blini (crepes) with red caviar, pirozhki (baked turnovers) filled with ground meat. It is unthinkable to skip the Ukrainian borscht or the fried (actually sautéed) mushrooms. The helpful waitresses would prevent you from making such flagrant omissions anyhow.

Rathbones

1702 Second Ave., near East 88th St.
Upper East Side, Manhattan
369-7361
Open: Mon.–Thurs. 5 P.M.–midnight, Fri. till 2 A.M., Sat.
  noon–1 A.M., Sun. noon–midnight
By subway: 4, 5, 6 to 86th St.
Average price per entree: $8
Alcohol: yes
Credit: AE, MC, V
Reservations: none
Classification: A Little Romance
Pièce de résistance: burger platter

Situated directly across the street from the cele-
brated literary watering hole Elaine's, Rathbones
may be on the wrong side of Second Avenue. But if
you're out to be fed rather than be seen, the choice
is elementary. Since the early seventies, Rathbones
has welcomed its neighbors on the Upper East Side
with reliable, low-priced, pub-style food and a con-
genial atmosphere. That combination is not always
so easy to find.

Beyond that, the greatest contribution a Manhattan pub can make to its community is a fat,
juicy steakburger. Rathbones has got a great one—
charred black on the outside, pretty in pink on the
inside, and delivered atop a toasted English muffin.
For $4.95 you get a hamburger platter with tomato,
lettuce, and shoestring French fries.

The beef doesn't stop there. The $8.25 London
broil, thin slices of tasty, tender meat topped with
mushrooms, and the $9.95 filet mignon are two of
the best beef bargains going. Among the other
entree choices are chicken cutlet parmigiana,

broiled fillet of sole almondine, and broiled chicken. Each comes with a salad and choice of fries or baked potato.

Rathbones also happens to be a great-looking pub, with sawdust on the floor, distinctive plaid tablecloths, brick walls, and a candle lantern at each table, adding a touch of romance to a brew and burger repast.

Ruben's Empanadas

64 Fulton St., near Gold St.
Financial District, Manhattan
962-7274
Open: Mon.–Sat. 7 A.M.–7 P.M.
By subway: 2, 3, 4, 5, J, M, R to Fulton St.; A, C to Broadway/Nassau St.
Average price per lunch special: $5.25
Alcohol: none
Credit: none
Reservations: none
Classification: Ethnic Treasure
Pièce de résistance: empanadas

When it comes to ethnic eat-to-the-beat pit stops, Ruben's Empanadas on Fulton Street is better than anything you're likely to find at the South Street Seaport's Fulton Mall and Pier 17. Ruben's freshly baked, homemade empanadas— doughy, half-moon pastry turnovers of South American origin—come with a choice of nine luscious fillings: beef, chili, chicken, broccoli, ham 'n' cheese, spinach, sausage, mushroom, and seafood (crab). Each one is a great bite, though I'm partial to the broccoli and the mildly spicy chili. Empanadas are $2 apiece ($2.50 for seafood). A lunch special with the soup of the day (lentil, split pea, beef vegetable, black bean, or Manhattan clam chowder), two empanadas, and a beverage is $5.50.

Primarily a takeout shop, Ruben's does have about a dozen stools for eating on the premises. I prefer to order one or two empanadas to go (always hot out of the oven) and enjoy them as I mill about the seaport, watched by jealous, hungry eyes.

Saigon

60 Mulberry St., near Bayard St.
Chinatown, Manhattan
227-8825
Open: Sun.–Thurs. 11:30 A.M.–10:30 P.M., Fri. & Sat.
  11 A.M.–11 P.M.
By subway: 6, J, M, N, Q, R to Canal St.; B, D, Q to
  Canal St.
Average price per nonseafood entree: $6
Alcohol: yes
Credit: AE, MC, V
Reservations: yes
Classification: Ethnic Treasure
Pièce de résistance: chicken with lemongrass

Saigon will pass quickly in your mind from the strange to the familiar. Many are drawn there at first to explore the exotic character of Vietnamese cooking, but the aesthetic manner in which the food is prepared and served, as well as its easy accessibility to American tastes, brings them back. I can't explain why the prices are so low and I didn't think it was a particularly wise idea to ask. I trust you'll be equally discreet.

This seems to be a menu where the first dish

listed in each category (appetizers, chicken, beef and pork, vegetable) is a house specialty. Or maybe I just got into the habit of reading the first entry, saying to myself, "That sounds good," and neglecting the alternatives. Atop the list of appetizers is Vietnamese spring rolls (cha gio)—four rolls in a thin, crisp, translucent rice wrapping, served with shredded carrot in a fish sauce; and barbecued shrimp on sugar cane (chao tom) topped with finely chopped peanuts and scallions.

My favorite entree is the chicken with lemongrass (ga xao xa), which is chunks of chicken heavily sauced in lemongrass and soy sauce. But I hope you choose to eat family-style so that you can also enjoy the Saigon special beef (thit bo nuong vi). The paper-thin slices of beef are sautéed to order right at your table on a portable burner. The meat cooks in a flash, maybe ten to twenty seconds depending on your preference—rare, medium, or well-done. As with the barbecued shrimp, the beef is topped with finely chopped peanuts and scallions, adding flavor and a slightly grainy texture. Friends and I are likely to fight over the most densely topped pieces. A nice vegetable ensemble, though less uniquely Vietnamese, is the vegetable delight—baby corn, pea pods, broccoli, carrots, tree mushrooms, bok choy, and cabbage in oyster sauce.

A few steps below street level, Saigon's cheerful dining room, filled with such reflective surfaces as mirrored walls and glass-topped red tablecloths, seats around sixty-five people. Only seafood entrees are priced over $8.25; seven rice vermicelli dishes are under $4.

Sam's

238 Court St., at Baltic St.
Cobble Hill, Brooklyn
(718) 596-3458
Open: Wed.–Mon. from about 11:30 A.M. to about
    10:30 P.M.
By subway: F to Bergen St.
Average price per entree: $8
Alcohol: yes
Credit: none
Reservations: yes
Classification: Ethnic Treasure
Pièce de résistance: pizza

While the movie *Moonstruck* was charming audiences at the Cobble Hill Cinema with its supposedly authentic slice of Brooklyn life, the real thing was playing right down the street. Sam's Restaurant, opened in 1930, is a homely but oh-so-homey Italian place struggling to cope in a drastically changing neighborhood. It's as enjoyably unsophisticated as drinking cheap red wine out of an orange juice glass or slurping a large plate of pasta and red sauce.

What really makes me feel like a king in Kings is Sam's incomparable brick-oven-baked pizzas: crispy, saucey pies with an ultrathin crust, divinely oozy mozzarella, and such toppings as mushrooms, eggplant, pepperoni, and garlic. *Bravissimo!* Play it again, Sam's, play it again and again.

Sapporo

152 West 49th St., near Seventh Ave.
Theater District, Manhattan
869-8972
Open: Mon.–Fri. 11:30 A.M.–midnight, Sat. & Sun. till
    11:00 P.M.
By subway: 1 to 50th St.; B, D, F, Q to 47th-50th
    Sts./Rockefeller Center; N, R to 49th St.
Average price per entree: $5
Alcohol: beer and saki
Credit: none
Reservations: none
Classification: Ethnic Treasure
Pièce de résistance: special ramen

Sapporo may be a little too grungy for pretheater
dining, but this Japanese greasy spoon on Tin Pan
Alley does possess its own degree of theatricality.
Diners seated at the ten-seat counter can see everything that goes on in the kitchen and it's a fasci-
nating show. These are not Benihana-type per-
formers behind the counter, but skilled short-order
cooks who sauté, fry, and boil heavily seasoned
food with speed and nonchalance.

Sapporo caters to its Japanese clientele with a
magazine/newspaper rack and a community bul-
letin board up front. Still, you don't need to speak
or read Japanese to enjoy the place. Most come in
for one of the ramen selections, which are combinations of noodles, meat, eggs, and vegetables in a
large bowl of soup, seasoned either with soy bean,
soy sauce, salt, or curry ($4 to $5). Those not in the
mood for soup might go for katsu-don (sort of a
pork omelet served over rice), pork ginger (pieces of
pork sautéed in ginger), or such standards as suki-

yaki, teriyaki, or tempura. Only tempura is priced over $4 and all come with rice and miso soup. For an appetizer, try sharing an order of gyoza (fried pork dumplings).

Small tables can be moved together to accommodate parties of all sizes, but you may wish to come in alone, grab a front-row seat at the counter, and get close enough to the action to feel the heat from blazing gas flames.

Sapporo East

245 East 10th St., at First Ave.
East Village, Manhattan
260-1330
Open: seven days 5 P.M.–12:45 A.M.
By subway: 6 to Astor Pl.; L to First Ave.
Average price per dinner: $8
Alcohol: beer and saki
Credit: none
Reservations: none
Classification: Ethnic Treasure
Pièce de résistance: sushi and tempura combination

Did you ever notice that when you ask someone what their favorite restaurant is, they mention some fancy place they go to once in a decade and not the corner ethnic joint they go to three, four times a week? I, for one, put a high value on a standby like the Sapporo East Japanese restaurant and sushi bar. The food is always good, the prices low, and the atmosphere in step with the neighborhood. Some funky East Villagers are in here so often, they ought to pay rent.

Unlike many other inexpensive Japanese restaurants, Sapporo East does not season its food to death. The teriyaki sauce, for example, is light and delicious. My top teriyaki pick is the salmon steak, but the chicken and beef teriyakis are good too. An even better beef dish is negimaki, sautéed beef rolled around scallions and sliced with sushi-like artistry.

The sushi and sashimi are consistently fresh and capably prepared; the combination deluxes are exceptional bargains ($8.50 with salad and miso soup). If ordering individual sushi rolls, three terrific choices are freshwater eel and cucumber, sea urchin, and salmon skin and cucumber. For those who prefer a little of this and a little that, the sushi-tempura combination is ideal.

Sapporo is not as style-conscious as most Japanese restaurants in town, but it is an upbeat and pleasant place to dine. But expect to overhear several conversations during the course of your dinner. The tables and chairs are packed as tightly as a sushi roll.

Sonali

326 East 6th St., near First Ave.
East Village, Manhattan
505-7517
Open: seven days noon–1 A.M.
By subway: 6 to Astor Pl.; F to Second Ave.
Average price per entree: $5
Alcohol: none
Credit: AE ($20 minimum)
Reservations: none
Classification: Ethnic Treasure
Pièce de résistance: lamb shree mangal

Hitting the East Village for Indian food is one of New York's great "Under $15" addictions. There are fifteen Indian restaurants on "Curry Lane," the south side of East 6th Street between First and Second Avenues. And most feature good food at prices that seem to predate color television.

I prefer Sonali, which gets the nod over Mitali because you can bring your own beer and wine. The restaurant is narrow and the tables and chairs are crammed together—I don't think there's enough legroom for anyone over six-foot-two—but Sonali is otherwise comfortable, quite pretty actually, and service is remarkably gracious considering the tight quarters.

Appetizers and breads can sometimes be the best part of an Indian dinner. At Sonali, well-prepared starters like vegetable somosa (deep-fried pastries), Sonali liver (chicken livers sautéed in onions and spices), and poori (puffed bread) will cost you a buck or two. Order several and pass them around.

Consistent meat and vegetarian entrees (mostly $4 to $6) are prepared to your desired level of spiciness. None are real scorchers; you can do that yourself by adding the fiery condiments. Some entree suggestions: lamb shree mangal (lamb cubes cooked with pineapple, almonds, sultana, and a mild cream sauce), jal piazi (a spicy vegetable dish seasoned with green pepper and spring onion), and sizzling chicken tikka (like the charcoal chicken tandoori, only prepared with boneless chunks of chicken breast, which makes it easier to share). All entrees are served with cabbage and choice of brown or saffron rice.

Occasionally there are short lines outside Sonali. Patient patrons are often served free hors d'oeuvres of vegetable fritters while they wait, as if the low prices weren't enough.

Sylvia's

328 Lenox Ave., near West 126th St.
Harlem, Manhattan
996-0660
Open: Mon.–Sat. 7:30 A.M.–10:30 P.M., Sun. 1 P.M.–7 P.M.
By subway: 2, 3 to 125th St.
Average price per entree: $8
Alcohol: yes
Credit: none
Reservations: not necessary
Classification: Ethnic Treasure
Pièce de résistance: barbecued ribs

Let's say it's your first visit to Sylvia's. Maybe you're not too familiar with soul food. You don't know what to order. Well, who better to ask than Sylvia herself?

"Do you like beef, pork, or poultry?" Sylvia Woods, proprietor of this New York institution, wants to know. "If you want beef, then it's the short ribs of beef. Pork, then barbecued ribs is tops. Chicken, have the smothered chicken. You can get fried chicken anytime." What if you happen to like all three? "Then leave it to me," says Sylvia, always ready to pamper guests. "Leave it to me."

If you leave it to Sylvia, you'll get a lot of everything, family-style. That's good news because you simply must get to know those sweet and spicy barbecued ribs and the soft chicken smothered in gravy. And I'm absolutely wild about three of her side vegetables: candied yams, collard greens, and black-eyed peas. There's nothing better to do with a fork. You'll probably be full after all that food, but you simply must find some reserve storage space for Sylvia's yummy sweet-potato pie.

Sylvia and Sylvia's have been the toast and taste of Harlem for over twenty-five years. The main dining area (there are four) is comfortable and informal; everyone is made to feel at home, even someone like me who's always finger-cleaning his plate. As Sylvia likes to say, "Y'all my favorite people."

Taro

20 East 47th St., near Madison Ave.
Midtown, Manhattan
986-7170
Open: Mon.–Fri. 7 A.M.–10 A.M., 11:30 A.M.–3 P.M., &
  5:30 P.M.–10 P.M.; Sat. noon–8 P.M.
By subway: 6 to 51st St.; B, D, F, Q to 47th-50th
  Sts./Rockefeller Center
Average price per entree: $5.50
Alcohol: yes
Credit: none
Reservations: none
Classification: Ethnic Treasure
Pièce de résistance: nameko udon

The people at Taro really know noodles and noodle soups, but they obviously don't have a yen for mastering the exchange rate. This Japanese restaurant is in midtown, yet prices for most lunch and dinner items are in the $5 neighborhood.

Taro's clean, modern, sharp-looking decor is nicely laid out with joinable tables for two, a four-seat noodle counter, and the centerpiece, a square communal table with a nine-seat perimeter. The lunch menu offers five choices of desirably understated, overstocked lamen noodle soups: vegetable, tofu, beef, seafood, or chicken. All are prepared either in a miso bean or soy-flavored soup base, with brussel sprouts, scallions, and shredded carrots. Two worthwhile nonsoup lunches are curry lamen, noodles topped with chopped clams in a heavy, beef-flavored curry sauce with carrots and potatoes, and salad lamen, a mixed plate of cold noodles with clams, shredded carrots, and lettuce in a ginger dressing, garnished with an orange slice and celery stick.

The dinner menu offers a larger variety of meat, vegetable, and seafood soups with either white, buckwheat, or egg noodles. I'm crazy about the wider white udon noodles. The namedo udon noodle soup includes Japanese mushrooms, grated white radish, and condiments of chopped scallions, dry seaweed, and pickles. One hint that Taro is superior to others of its kind is the way the shrimp and vegetable tempura appetizer is presented. It comes on a napkin-lined bamboo tray, an act of courage because the napkin shows how greasy the tempura is, or in Taro's case, is not.

An alluring alternative to everything noodle is the okonomi yaki, a Japanese-style crepe filled with cabbage, shredded carrots, and choice of squid, octopus, or beef, then topped with finely chopped seaweed, mayonnaise, and sweet-and-pungent tonkatsu sauce. The cost of this delicacy is $5, or a little over 600 yen.

Thai Village

133 West 3rd St., near Sixth Ave.
Greenwich Village, Manhattan
254-9513
Open: Mon. noon–10 P.M., Tues.–Sun. till 11:30 P.M.
By subway: A, B, C, D, E, F, Q to West 4th St.
Average price per nonseafood entree: $7.50
Alcohol: beer and wine
Credit: AE, DC, MC, V
Reservations: none
Classification: Ethnic Treasure
Pièce de résistance: pad Thai

Diners who do not apply the "no pain, no gain" principle to spicy cuisines will appreciate the milder Thai cooking at Thai Village. The food, like a piano trio performing next door at the Blue Note, always swings but rarely burns. That's because curry arranger Khun Preeya uses chili peppers sparingly, if at all.

Thai Village's small dining room, with its eight glass-topped tables, candlelight, hanging plants, and soft music, is a tranquil and unassuming refuge from the kinetic energy of Washington Square. All pungency is reserved for the food, which is instantly apparent in tom-yum-goong, a very sour and not-very-hot shrimp soup with lemongrass, lime, and mushrooms, and yum-goong, a cold appetizer of shrimp tossed with lime, cucumber, and Thai dressing.

Two can't-miss entrees are mas-mann ($7.95), tender, marinated beef cubes in peanut sauce and Thai curry, and pad Thai ($5.95), thin Thai noodles sautéed in a multitextured mix of egg, shrimp, bean curd, ground peanuts, scallions, and bean sprouts. Also worth considering, perhaps with a request for added pepper punch, are moo-ga-thiem-prik-Thai, pork sautéed with garlic and pepper, and gang gai, chicken sautéed with Thai curry, pepper, coconut sauce, and bamboo shoots. All nonnoodle dishes are served with rice.

Tierras Colombianas

82-18 Roosevelt Ave., near 83rd St.
Jackson Heights, Queens
(718) 426-8868
Open: Mon.–Thurs. 11 A.M.–11 P.M., Fri.–Sun. till midnight
By subway: 7 to 82nd St.
Average price per entree: $6
Alcohol: none
Credit: none
Reservations: none
Classification: Ethnic Treasure
Pièce de résistance: country plate

Undereating and overspending at Tierras Co-lombianas are as rare as a snowstorm in Bogota. What is abundant at this Colombian family restau-rant, one of several in Jackson Heights, is the hearty and heavy native food. Not much English is spoken, but there is an English menu to help those who don't speak or understand Spanish.

Newcomers to the cuisine can order the hefty country plate of grilled beef, fried pork, egg, plan-tain, avocado, rice, and beans as a complete sampler. I prefer the pork to the thin, garlicky grilled steak, but you ought to try both. Pass on the fried porgie unless you must have fish.

It's hard to believe that anyone orders a large bowl of chunky soup as an appetizer. These delicious meals-in-a-bowl du jour ($3.50) may contain fish, tripe, oxtail, beef, yucca, plantain, potatoes, corn, or a number of other good vegetables and things.

Complementing the food and the bright, musical, folksy flavor inside Tierras Colombianas are the tropical fruit milk shakes, which are fast becoming a New York summer standard. TC's are among the best I've had.

Tom's Restaurant

782 Washington Ave., at Sterling Pl.
Prospect Heights, Brooklyn
(718) 636-9738
Open: Mon.–Sat. 5 A.M.–4:30 P.M.
By subway: 2, 3 to Eastern Parkway/Brooklyn Museum
Average price per breakfast: $2
Alcohol: none
Credit: none
Reservations: none
Classification: Positively NYC
Pièce de résistance: egg cream

Three blocks north of the Brooklyn Museum, minutes from the Brooklyn Botanic Garden, the Brooklyn Public Library, and Prospect Park, and miles from the anxieties of city life is a precious New York-style luncheonette called Tom's Restaurant.

It's a neighborly place where people breakfast and lunch out, or maybe just sip a coffee or soda, to feel at home.

The classic, circa-1936 shop has a marble counter, striped booths, homespun wall hangings, and best of all, Gus, an extraordinarily friendly man who wants everything to be right. Gus takes care of the people he likes and that includes almost anybody who walks into the shop.

Stop in for eggs with delicious, just-greasy-enough home fries or challah French toast for breakfast, any one of a number of reliable sandwiches for lunch, or perhaps your pick of the definitive sodas: ice cream soda, egg cream, or lime rickey. A lime rickey is what Cherry 7-Up should but doesn't taste like. It's made to order with cherry syrup, fresh lime, and soda. Sip a tall, ice-cold glass and you'll have discovered the most effective antidote for New York's hot and muggy summer days.

Tony's Souvlaki

28-44 31st St., near 30th Ave.
Astoria, Queens
(718) 728-3638
Open: Sun.–Thurs. 11 A.M.–midnight, Fri. & Sat. till 1 A.M.
By subway: N to 30th Ave.
Average price per pita sandwich: $2.50
Alcohol: beer and wine
Credit: none
Reservations: none
Classification: Ethnic Treasure
Pièce de résistance: gyro sandwich

You'd know what Tony's Souvlaki stand and restaurant looks like even if you'd never been there—checkered tablecloths, tacky brickwork, char-broiler and rotisserie up front—but you wouldn't be able to imagine how flavorful and satisfying this type of Greek food can be.

The souvlaki, tender chunks of marinated, char-broiled lamb, is first-rate, yet clearly second choice to the gyro meat, which is pink, tender, juicy, and delish—the best in town. A third choice is the chicken kebab, which is decent though not quite in the same league. Each is $2.50 wrapped in pita with the works, or $5.50 for an enormous platterful with Greek salad, fries, and pita. A large bowl of the commendable Greek salad, enough for two, is only $2.

Is Tony's Souvlaki worth a special trip from Manhattan? My first instinct says no, but it's really a question that gyro lovers must decide for themselves. You could do worse.

Tortilla Flats

767 Washington St., at West 12th St.
Greenwich Village, Manhattan
243-1053
Open: Mon.–Thurs. noon–midnight, Fri. noon–1 A.M.,
    Sat. 5 P.M.–1 A.M., Sun. 3 P.M.–11:30 P.M.
By subway: A, C, E to 14th St.
Average price per entree: $8
Alcohol: yes
Credit: none
Reservations: for groups of eight or more
Classification: Funky Casual
Pièce de résistance: carnitas Colorado

You've read the John Steinbeck novel! You've seen the Spencer Tracy movie! Now get set for the boldest adaptation of all—Tortilla Flats, the restaurant! In 1983, rockabilly restaurateur Stan Tankursely, hit-and-run architect of jumpin' jukebox joints, trashed the original story and setting of Tortilla Flat to cook up a degraded tale of Tex-Mex partydom in the West Village. Over eighteen hundred performances later, they are still taking names at the door of Tortilla Flats.

Why? The initial excitement of the wacky decor—part retro-diner, part honky-tonk, part used-record store in Tijuana—may be played out, but funky-casual diners have gotten used to the loungy atmosphere and the Tex-Mex fun food. I think the kitchen has actually improved over the years. The chile con queso, tortilla chips with a dip of melted cheese and chopped jalapeño peppers ($3.95), is a yummy appetizer for two to four players. And though combo plates tend to be more reliable than the more-challenging house specialties, the carnitas Colorado, luscious shredded pork burritos with hot ranchero (beans and chili) sauce; and chile rellenos, stuffed green chili peppers covered with corn meal, then deep-fried, are $7.95 knockouts. One minor disappointment is the pollo verde, which is prepared a little bit differently at every Mexican restaurant. At Tortilla Flats, you get a nice piece of chicken, but the green chili and tomatillo (green tomato) topping is more of a relish than a sauce and no cause for a fiesta.

For dessert, the deep-fried tortilla flats, sort of like a Mexican cheese blintz, is nothing you need to try.

Totonno Pizzeria Napoletano

1524 Neptune Ave., near West 16th St.
Coney Island, Brooklyn
(718) 372-8606
Open: Fri.–Sun. 2 P.M.–9 P.M. (call first)
By subway: B, D, F, N to Stillwell Ave./Coney Island
Average price per pizza: $8
Alcohol: beer and wine
Credit: none
Reservations: none
Classification: Ethnic Treasure
Pièce de résistance: pizza

In walking distance though quite removed from the carnival amusements at Coney Island is an old-fashioned shop where New York's finest pizza is baked. Totonno Pizzeria Napoletano was opened in the early twenties by Anthony Totonno, a disciple of Gennaro Lombardi, America's original pizzaiollo. Today it is Anthony's son Jerry who orchestrates these definitive masterpizzas.

Totonno's coal-heated brick oven turns out a divinely crisp yet light crust—thin and slightly charred on the edges—without daring to overcook the dreamy, sliced homemade mozzarella or the sweet tomato sauce. Extra toppings are limited, but this isn't a pie you want to camouflage. A house specialty is pizza bianca (white pizza)—no tomatoes.

"The best way (to top a tomato pizza) is just mozzarella or anchovies, but not both," says Jerry Totonno. "And usually, if you get three pies, one has to be white pizza." Trust this man; do not come here and tell him how they do things where you come from. This would be like telling Leonardo that what the Mona Lisa needs is a big, toothy grin.

Jerry's quaint shop seats about forty. The tin walls are painted powder blue, as are two extra-large booths that seat six comfortably, eight who really like each other. One prominent wall hanging is a framed front page from the long defunct *Daily Mirror*: "War Over; M'Arthur to Rule Japs."

Don't expect much in the way of friendly service. The staff behaves like artists—deeply concerned with the preparation of the canvas, but aloof about its sale. That and old age explains why Totonno's has such limited and unreliable hours.

Trattoria Pietro & Vanessa

23 Cleveland Pl., near Spring St.
Little Italy, Manhattan
226-9764
Open: Mon.–Fri. noon–11 P.M., Sat. 4 P.M.–11 P.M., Sun. 4 P.M.–10 P.M.
By subway: 6 to Spring St.
Average price per entree: $7.50
Alcohol: yes
Credit: AE, MC, V
Reservations: for parties of five or more
Classification: Ethnic Treasure
Pièce de résistance: spaghetti filletto

Trattoria Pietro & Vanessa, Little Italy's finest "Under $15" eatery, is cherished for the simple pleasures that abound within. Glasses of white wine in an unadorned backyard garden. Baskets of semolina rolls. Forkfuls of fresh pasta in delicate sauces. What better way to spend a summer evening in New York?

There are no secrets about P&V's fourteen pasta dishes (all $6.95): They're fresh, basic, poetic. Spaghetti filletto (tomato sauce with diced prosciutto and onion) is a standout. Ask the waitress if she can have the filletto prepared for you with orrechiette (small pasta "ears") in place of spaghetti and the addition of mozzarella. Linguine vongole (clam sauce), rigatoni quattro formaggi (four cheeses), and fusilli primavera are all delightful, and I think you'll like the understated veal and chicken entrees too (mostly $7.95 to $8.95).

For starters, be sure to have a garden-fresh salad—perhaps arugula if it's in season. You might also share a plate of calamari fritti ($7.95), served with a thin, peppery tomato sauce.

Even native New Yorkers may need walking directions to Pietro & Vanessa. It's situated a few blocks away from the heart of Little Italy on Cleveland Place, an obscure, two-block-long street. Go to the corner of Lafayette and Spring Streets and that will lead you into Cleveland Place and the joys of moonlit pasta.

Tutta Pasta

26 Carmine St., near Bleecker St.
Greenwich Village, Manhattan
242-4871
Open: Mon.–Thurs. 11:30 A.M.–10:30 P.M., Fri. & Sat.
  till 11:30 P.M.
By subway: A, B, C, D, E, F, Q to West 4th St.
Average price per pasta: $5.95
Alcohol: none
Credit: none
Reservations: none
Classification: Ethnic Treasure
Pièce de résistance: fettucine filetti di pomadori

Tutta Pasta is what I'd call a "little-too-much"
cafe. There's a little too much chopped garlic in the
linguine and white clam sauce (with a half-dozen
fresh clams), a little too much prosciutto in the
fettucine filetti di pomadori (tomato sauce with
onions and prosciutto), a little too much to eat in a
plate of vegetable ravioli in a house sauce of tomatoes, heavy cream, mushrooms, and peas—all of
which I like a little too much. Same goes for the
heavy-on-the-vegetables pasta primavera and the
delightfully delicate tortellini (you can get a box to
take home next door). I think the tortellini goes
best with the tomato-and-cream sauce.

Most of the eighteen quality homemade pastas at
this forty-seat restaurant, a new extension of the
popular Tutta Pasta takeout store, are $5.95—not a
bad excuse for locals to close their kitchen for an
evening.

For an appetizer, I prefer the house salad to the
routine hot mixed antipasto. There's a nice selection of pastries for dessert, but unfortunately no

espresso or cappuccino. You may want to skip dessert here and go to one of the more atmospheric cafes nearby.

The room itself is pleasantly understated, more plain vanilla than primavera. Space is a little tight, which is why I find it odd that the waitresses go from table to table with a four-foot-long pepper mill. This is like swinging a baseball bat in a telephone booth. Can't blame them, I suppose, for trying a little too much.

Two Boots

37 Avenue A, near East 3rd St.
East Village, Manhattan
505-5450
Open: Tues.–Sun. noon–midnight
By subway: F to 2nd Ave.
Average price per entree: $7
Alcohol: beer and wine
Credit: none
Reservations: none
Classification: Funky Casual
Pièce de résistance: crawfish pizza

You're sure to get a kick out of Two Boots and its trendy-funky-tacky-nutty-ethnic-diner-retread design. Even more eccentric than the decor is the cuisine. Two Boots, named after the world's two great geographical boots, Italy and Louisiana, is New York's first Italian-Cajun pizzeria and restaurant.

Actually, Italian-Cajun hybrid restaurants are not uncommon in the bayou. And in the East Village, where anything goes, Two Boots makes this intermarriage work. Their pizza basics are firmly established—thin, crispy crust, garlic-laden tomato sauce, and soft, creamy mozzarella. But then they add some radical toppings: jalapeños, roasted peppers, shrimp, soppressata. I tried and liked the crawfish pizza ($6 for an individual pie) and that's a difficult confession for a pizza purist to make in print.

After an appetizer of fried calamari or Cajun garlic bread, you might go for one of the po' boys (hero sandwiches). They're assembled on ultra-crusty Italian bread coated with a choice of garlic or sweet-pepper mayo. Two are standouts: the roasted vegetable ($4.95), made with mushrooms, pesto, and artichoke hearts, and the fried catfish.

Recommended among the entrees ($5.95 to $8.75): the garlicky fettucine primacasa (in a sauce of garlic butter, red pepper, kale, broccoli, and parmesan cheese); the hot and spicy shrimp Mosca, served in a cast-iron skillet with bread crumbs, garlic, herbs, and parmesan cheese; and chicken à la grande, roasted in garlic, rosemary, and Cinzano for a predictably heavy yet flavorful result.

I'm tellin' ya, an Italian-Cajun wedding is a lively affair.

Two Toms

255 Third Ave., near Union St.
Park Slope, Brooklyn
(718) 875-8689
Open: Tues.–Sun. 5:30 P.M.–9:30 P.M.
By subway: N, R to Union St.
Average price per entree: $6
Alcohol: beer and wine

Credit: none
Reservations: necessary on weekends
Classification: Ethnic Treasure
Pièce de résistance: breast of chicken rollatini

If Two Toms is, more or less, your typical neighborhood Italian restaurant, why do people keep coming back from near and far? It sure isn't the decor. Plain, wood-paneled walls and drab brown tablecloths please only by their unassuming simplicity. It can't be the entertainment. There are plenty of good shows to watch on that black-and-white TV set, but that's hardly reason enough to drive in from Staten Island. And no, it is not the presence of two men named Tom. There was actually only one, Tom Giordano, and he passed away fifteen years ago.

Two Toms is special for the simple reasons that less is more and more is less. That is, less showy frills allow for a more convivial atmosphere and more hearty food is served for less money. Two Toms lives by the theme of this book: *Abondanza without Arroganza.*

The current owner is Giordano's brother-in-law, Jimmy Catapano. His daughter Angela is the chef; son Anthony—pronounced ANT-nee—is the only waiter. That's a family business.

There's no menu. Anthony tells newcomers about his sister's specialties, mostly traditional southern Italian veal, chicken, seafood, and pasta dishes. Take notice of the veal or pork chops sitting on an adjacent table before ordering. They're tender, juicy, and probably too large for most human beings. Mortals may prefer the breast of chicken rollatini (chicken rolled over prosciutto and ri-

131

cotta), the baked ziti (with mozzarella and eggplant), or shrimp scampi. Meat dishes come with a
choice of salad or ziti in tomato sauce. Only steak is
priced over $8.

No desserts are served, but anisette is *gratuito.*
Anyway, with all this food, few have reason to
complain.

"If they do complain," says Anthony, "it's usually
'cause we don't cook it like their mothers. Everybody thinks his mother is the best cook in the
world."

Two Toms makes a solid case for everybody
being wrong.

V & T Pizzeria

1024 Amsterdam Ave., near Cathedral Pkwy. (West
110th St.)
Morningside Heights, Manhattan
663-1708
Open: Tues.–Sun. 11:30 A.M.–11:45 P.M.
By subway: 1 to Cathedral Pkwy.
Average price per pizza: $6.50
Alcohol: beer and wine
Credit: none
Reservations: none
Classification: Positively NYC
Pièce de résistance: cheese pizza

People who describe V & T as the pizzeria near
Columbia University have got it backwards. Columbia University is the school near V & T Pizzeria.

For over forty years V & T has nourished Columbia students and their neighbors in Morningside Heights with satisfying, inexpensive, "red

sauce" Italian food. The main event, however, has always been pizza. V & T is one of the only places left in New York where the dough is still mixed by hand to retain its air pockets. This results in a softer, lighter crust. Even more memorable than the crust is the oily mozzarella, which is not, as is often believed, a sure-fire sign of inferiority. Pizzas made with full cream, top-shelf mozzarella are naturally "buttery" and should not be confused with corner slice shops that use low-grade cheeses and add oil.

Besides students, V & T also draws its share of the hungry and famous: Jacklyn Smith, Penny Marshall, Paul Simon, Art Garfunkel. Jack Nicholson was stood up there once by two gals, so he shared a pie with his chauffeur in his limousine. That just goes to prove: No one is lonely with a good pizza.

Veronica Ristorante Italiano

240 West 38th St., near Seventh Ave.
Garment Center, Manhattan
764-4770
Open: Mon.–Fri. 6 A.M.–4 P.M.
By subway: 1, 2, 3, A, C, E, R, N to 42nd St.
Average price per lunch entree: $7
Alcohol: beer and wine
Credit: none
Reservations: none
Classification: Ethnic Treasure
Pièce de résistance: eggplant rollatini

The Garment Center sophisticate makes the decision to lunch at Veronica at approximately 11:07 A.M. By that time, the morning mail has already come in without the overdue purchase orders, a shipment of dresses from Hong Kong has turned up in Tennessee, and the office air conditioner is on for the first time in ten years, even though the temp outside is six below.

This is Veronica time, time for a heap of hearty Italian food served weekdays in this deceptively routine-looking, cafeteria-style deli restaurant. Handwritten sheets posted at the beginning of the line announce the daily specials: chicken chiapponata (chicken in white wine with roasted peppers, mushrooms, tomato, and capers), risotto marinaio (rice with seafood), cannelloni Veronica (crepes filled with seafood, ricotta cheese, and spinach), eggplant rollatini (eggplant stuffed with ricotta cheese and topped with mozzarella and mushroom-tomato sauce). Nonetheless, few order anything by name. Most study the steam table like the inside of their home refrigerators before ordering "the green one with the tomatoes and those little olive things." The dishes are always satisfying, often inspiring, never understated.

An absolute delight at breakfast is the egg casserole, filled with ham and cheese or assorted vegetables. My only disappointment at Veronica occurred during a visit one January afternoon. I was three-quarters done with a plate of sole florentina when I got up to grab a cup of water. When I returned to the table, my plate had already been cleared by an overly efficient busboy. Never again, I promised myself, as I wiped away a tear and walked east towards Seventh Avenue.

Veselka

144 Second Ave., at East 9th St.
East Village, Manhattan
228-9682
Open: Sun.–Thurs. 7 A.M.–12:30 A.M., Fri. & Sat. till
1 A.M.
By subway: 6 to Astor Pl.
Average price per entree: $6.50
Alcohol: none
Credit: none
Reservations: none
Classification: Positively NYC
Pièce de résistance: deluxe meat combination dinner

Veselka is a cup of strong coffee and a bowl of
hearty soup to stimulate and soothe the hopes and
dreams of East Villagers. This corner coffee shop is
not pretty, but its solid Ukrainian-Polish food, low
prices, and frank informality attract that extraordinary mix of characters—artists, students, elder
Eastern Europeans—that gives the neighborhood
its abundance of creative energy. (This Second
Avenue mix is portrayed in a ten-by-twelve-foot
burlesque mural outside the restaurant.) Sometimes it seems as though every Veselka regular
should be either writing a screenplay or having one
written about them.

The best value on Veselka's "pierogi plus" menu
has to be the deluxe meat combo ($6.50): cup of
soup (vegetable gets the nod here, but you can't
miss with cabbage, mushroom barley, split pea,
borscht, or lentil), green salad (boring!), kielbasa,

fabulous stuffed cabbage in chopped-mushroom gravy and three pierogi (meat, potato, and cabbage) topped with sautéed onions. For breakfast or whenever, the soft but not-too-thick banana wheatcakes ($3.25) taste great from first bite to last.

As a sign of the times, Veselka is now serving Ben & Jerry's Ice Cream (Eastern European goes Eastern Vermont) for dessert. Following the "when in Rome" principle, I prefer a piece of poppy seed cake, although their new practice of heating it in the microwave rather than on the griddle is unsatisfactory. My other minor complaint about Veselka is the limited legroom at the winding counter. I'm not coordinated enough to eat borscht sideways.

Wine and Apples

117 West 57th St., near Sixth Ave.
Midtown, Manhattan
246-9009
Open: seven days noon–midnight
By subway: 1, A, C, D to 59th St./Columbus Circle; N, R, Q to 57th St.
Average price per entree: $6.50
Alcohol: yes
Credit: AE, MC, V
Reservations: not necessary
Classification: A Little Romance
Pièce de résistance: moussaka

Concerts at Carnegie Hall. Ballets at City Center. Classic films at the Biograph Cinema. These are the days of Wine and Apples, a most unexpected oasis for economical dining on West 57th Street. Talk about peculiar, this has got to be the world's only Greek-German-American restaurant–wine 'n' cheese bar.

Wine and Apples is probably what a European country tavern/wine cellar would look like if situated in a high-rent district. For a flicker of romance, a candle, held at each table by an empty wine bottle subbing for a candlestick, illuminates the special for two: carafe of wine, sliced apples, and port salut cheese for $10.50.

Greek offerings like moussaka (a casserole of eggplant and lamb with a soufflé-like topping), the oversized country salad bowl with feta cheese, and, if available as a special, pastitsio (macaroni and meat casserole–the Greek lasagna) are probably the best bets. The soft, tasty, greaseless pastitsio ought to be on the daily menu.

The German dishes–wursts, wiener schnitzel, smoked loin of pork, etc.–are certainly no embarrassment. The schnitzel (paper-thin cutlets) is saved by two excellent sides: German-style cabbage and home fries. Two side attractions that almost qualified for pièce de résistance honors are the lentil soup and rice pudding.

Wo Hop

17 Mott St., near Pell St.
Chinatown, Manhattan
962-8617
Open: daily 24 hours
By subway: 6, J, M, N, Q, R to Canal St.; B, D, Q to Grand St.
Average price per entree: $4

137

Alcohol: none
Credit: none
Reservations: none
Classification: Positively NYC
Pièce de résistance: duck wonton soup

Two considerations come into play when choosing Wo Hop as a dining destination: time and money. Wo Hop, the leader among Chinatown's notorious down 'n' dirty restaurants, is open twenty-four hours for people who don't need to look at their watch to decide whether they're hungry or not. For a post-party, post-clubbing, post-anything case of the munchies, Wo Hop gets the call, especially if you've only got a few crumpled bills in your pocket. You can eat an awful lot of tasty food at Wo Hop for $3 or $4.

Though some may dismiss Wo Hop as just another greasy chopstick, it deserves credit as a master of noodle nuance. The lo mein and chow fun dishes ($2.45 and up) and the wonton soups (try duck wonton) are really quite good. The fried noodles are legendary. Where Wo Hop seems to go wrong is with preparations that rely heavily on meat. You probably shouldn't be eating those at 4 A.M. anyway.

Be prepared to wait on line along the staircase leading down to Wo Hop, even during early morning hours. There're a lot of hungry night owls in the naked city.

Wong Kee

113 Mott St., near Hester St.
Chinatown, Manhattan
966-1160
Open: seven days 11 A.M.–9:45 P.M.
By subway: 6, J, M, N, R to Canal St.; B, D, Q to Grand
   St.
Average price per entree: $7
Alcohol: none
Credit: none
Reservations: none
Classification: Ethnic Treasure
Pièce de résistance: hong shiu chicken

Many good friendships have been broken in
Chinatown because it's so difficult to agree on a
place to eat. That's why it's important to know
about Wong Kee, a place everybody likes and more
than a few of us love. It happens to be situated on
the outskirts of Chinatown proper, one block
north of Canal Street.

Nothing about Wong Kee's new design suggests
that it is a Chinese restaurant. The bright yellow,
green, blue, and red colors make it appear as
though Fisher-Price did the redecorating. The
room is noisy and crammed and everything moves
too fast. But remember, it's Chinatown. People
come to eat, not to sit back and be mellow.

Some of Wong Kee's meat specialties are so
flavorful they taste as though they've been mari-
nating since the days of the Last Emperor. Two fine
examples: wong kee steak—long, tender strips of
broiled beef over broccoli and black bean sauce—
and chicken sizzling with black bean sauce, garlic,
ginger, and scallions. One dish that always amazes

first-timers is hong shiu chicken, an enormous plate of spring chicken fried to a innocent shade of golden brown and served over shredded bamboo, Chinese mushrooms, and vegetables. The crispy coating could not be less greasy; the chicken could not be more tender. Also recommended: won kung shrimp, with preserved bean curd and hot pepper; chicken with cashew nuts, in a mildly spicy sauce; and the succulent, too-hot-to-handle barbecued ribs, an absolute must. Soups are reliable too. And the best news is that nothing mentioned here is priced over $7.75, including tax.

If Wong Kee has one drawback, it's the speedy service. Entrees usually arrive at your table while you're halfway through the soup or ribs. I suggest you order soup first and wait till it's served before ordering entrees. Then attack!

Zula

1260 Amsterdam Ave., at West 122nd St.
Morningside Heights, Manhattan
663-1670
Open: seven days noon–midnight
By subway: 1 to 125th St.
Average price per entree: $5.75
Alcohol: yes
Credit: AE, MC, V
Reservations: accepted but not necessary
Classification: Ethnic Treasure
Pièce de résistance: alitcha

Hand-to-mouth dining for a hand-to-mouth budget attracts a nice mix of Columbia University students and their neighbors to this relaxed Ethiopian bistro. Zula is modestly decorated with wood paneling, latticework, and tavern chairs, but what entrances diners is the blend of candlelight with the hypnotic hum of native music played dimly over small speakers.

The gracious waitresses will gladly demonstrate for you the customary way of eating without utensils, which can be both fun and sensuous. All foods are hand-eaten with injera, a sour, spongy, crepelike bread that lines the large pizza pan on which dishes are served. Alitcha is a delicious lamb specialty with a buttery sauce of onions and green pepper. Tsebehio derho, chicken simmered in a spicy red sauce with hard-boiled eggs and yogurt, is a little difficult to handle, but worth the trouble. Order also the special tebsie (beef cubes sautéed with peppers, onions, and spices) and the shiro (chick-peas flavored with a special prepared butter, onions, and spices) and you'll have a rather complete sampling of Zula's fine East African cooking. Entrees are priced from $4.25 to $6.95.

Strictly Noshing

Chinatown Ice Cream Factory

65 Bayard St.
Chinatown, Manhattan
608-4170

Did you know that lychee, red bean, green tea, ginger, and almond cookie were ice cream flavors? They're well worth trying at this unique Chinatown scoop shop.

Christie's

334 Flatbush Ave.
Park Slope, Brooklyn
(718) 636-9746

Christie's bakery has mastered the Jamaican beef patty. The flaky shell and spicy ground-meat filling of their patties combine for an exhilarating nosh — a New York eat-it-'n'-beat-it classic. Each comes with cocoa bread, a supersoft bun made with a formula that includes butter, not chocolate. Another Christie's West Indian specialty is coconut bread (a.k.a. coconut turnovers). These are large, soft buns with a gooey filling of coconut and sugar. Catch one right out of the oven and you'll swoon.

Fung Wong Bakery

30 Mott St.
Chinatown, Manhattan
267-4037

At the tantalizing Fung Wong Bakery, yellow-and-red shoe boxes are piled from floor to ceiling, filled with such likable Chinese goodies as noodle cake, lotus seed moon cake, and almond cookies. You can make your selections from the glass display cases.

Gloria Pizza

40-20 Main St.
Flushing, Queens
(718) 359-8844

Look out for pizza burn! The soupy sauce and cheese that float freely on the thin crust will sear your palate if you don't let it cool.

Karl Droge

6508 Sixth Ave., at 66th St.
Bay Ridge, Brooklyn
(718) 833-1407

You can tell summer is near when the kids start lining up outside this eighty-year-old ice cream stand. Karl Droge serves up generous portions of the finest soft ice cream in the city—either on a cone or in a cup with superior toppings. The hot fudge and butterscotch are truly hot, not luke-warm; the walnut topping is made with maple-flavored syrup, not corn syrup.

Knish Nosh

145 Fourth Ave.
East Village, Manhattan
529-4910

101-02 Queens Blvd.
Forest Hills, Queens
(718) 897-5554

A Knish Nosh knish is a knish on the brink. The delicate pastry shell is ill-suited for the job of containing its mashed potato, kasha, or chopped liver filling. Catastrophic collapse must be avoided by instantly sinking your teeth into this handful of goodness. A better knish there is knot.

L & B Spumoni Gardens

2725 86th St.
Bensonhurst, Brooklyn
(718) 372-8400

Watching the L & B pizzamen—all of them Brooklyn celebs—pull one of those steaming, Sicilian trays out of the oven and cut it into twenty-four square slices is a hypnotic prelude to that dreamy first bite: an explosion of tomatoey flavor. The dough, cooked soft enough in the middle, hard on the bottom, is first topped with mozzarella, followed by a pool of zesty tomato sauce and a thin layer of grated cheese. Next door to the pizzeria, L & B's ice cream stand serves up the best spumoni in town, a smooth, richly flavored swirl of chocolate, pistachio, and vanilla.

Mamoun's Falafel

119 MacDougal St.
Greenwich Village, Manhattan
674-9246

This mysterious, diminutive spot may have opened as a Mamoun for the misbegotten, but a legitimate falafel has been prepared here for the last fifteen years—spiced and fried just right, then stuffed into pita with lettuce, tomato, and tahini (mild sesame dressing). Hot sauce is optional.

Moishe's Falafel

West 46thSt. at Sixth Ave.
Midtown, Manhattan

A great food cart with a team of five preparing the finest falafel in midtown. Each pita is packed with spicy, undry, falafel with a perfect fried coating, along with lettuce, tomato, peppers, tahini dressing, and optional hot sauce. If the weather is nice, you can eat your falafel at the glorious International Paper Plaza. If the weather is nasty, the number at the nearest pay phone is 560-8588. Just ask the person who answers if Moishe's is open.

Nunzio's

2155 Hylan Blvd.
Staten Island
(718) 667-9647

Among by-the-slice pizzerias, Nunzio's, a short, stucco shack on Staten Island's main thoroughfare, bakes the city's triumphant triangle: light, thin, crisp crust, extra-fresh sauce, top-shelf mozzarella with a salty dash of Romano cheese. Order a slice with sausage and you won't be able to see the cheese.

Original Souvlaki

102 MacDougal St.
Greenwich Village, Manhattan
982-2838

Original Souvlaki is known more for its striped awning and outdoor counter than its name and sitdown restaurant. The gyro is the meatiest in Manhattan: tender, juicy meat carved off the rotisserie and stuffed into pita with the works. Also ready-to-go: shish kebab and Italian sausage with peppers and onions.

Peppino's Pizza

4701 White Plains Rd.
The Bronx
994-7543

The IRT subway points upward to Peppino's, the end of the line for calzoni: baked cocoons of pizza dough filled with fresh meats, veggies, and cheeses. The first bite to reach those fillings is an explosion of juicy flavors. I usually put my money down on the number five calzone — veal, peppers, onions, mushrooms, and mozzarella.

Piatti Pronto

---

34 West 56th St.
Midtown, Manhattan
315-4800

Come to the four-seat espresso bar at this outstanding Italianate take-out shop for panninni, delicious grilled sandwiches. The one with ham, provolone, and honey mustard melts on the grill and in your mouth.

Seaport Fries

---

11 Fulton St.
South Street Seaport, Manhattan

This stand at the Food Hall on the second floor of the South Street Seaport's Fulton Market fries tall, slender, fresh-cut Idaho potatoes and sweet potatoes to golden-brown perfection. You might try topping them with vinegar instead of catsup.

Stromboli

---

83 St. Mark's Pl.
East Village, Manhattan
673-3691

The impressive variety of ethnic eateries in the East Village won't satisfy an irrepressible urge for pizza. Better bop in here for a slice on the run. The cheese is moist, the crust firm, and the sweet, savory sauce hits the mark!

The Wurst

2832 Broadway
Morningside Heights, Manhattan
749-6190

This techno-pop, fast-food import from L.A. doesn't sell wursts, wieners, sausages, or franks; they're tubular steaks. There are nine varieties — all fat, juicy, spicy, snappy, mesquite-grilled, and served on a robust poppy-seed roll with a nice selection of mustards and toppings. The cute corner shop, with three tables-for-two, a dozen counter stools, and a jukebox, is a cheerful pit stop worthy of duplication around town.

The Best of the Best

From babka to wursts, a nosh-lover's checklist of the best bites in town.

kosher corned beef	Bernstein-On-Essex St.	8
macaroni and cheese	Horn & Hardart	
	Dine-O-Mat	55
mashed potatoes	Broadway Diner	10
Nova Scotia salmon	Carnegie Delicatessen	17
onion loaf	Dallas BBQ	30
onion rings	Moondance Diner	93
pancakes	Good Enough to Eat	46
pasta	Cucina Stagionale	26
pastrami	Carnegie Delicatessen	17
pastries	Patisserie Lanciani	103
pierogis	Christine's	22
peanut butter	Country Life	24
pizza pie	Totonno Pizzeria	
	Napoletano	125
pizza slice	Nunzio's	148
potato latkes	Moisha's Luncheonette	91
rotisserie chicken	El Pollo	36
ribs	Sylvia's	116
rice pudding	Marti Kebab	89
samosas	Sonali	114
soft ice cream	Karl Droge	146
soups	Grand Dairy	47
spumoni	L&B Spumoni Gardens	147
sundaes	Eddie's Sweet Shop	34
sushi	Sapporo East	113
tuna fish sandwich	Eisenberg Sandwich Shop	35
wonton soup	Wo Hop	137
wursts	The Wurst	151

Index by Location

Financial District

Chinatown

Lower East Side/East Village

Little Italy/SoHo/TriBeCa

Greenwich Village

Eastside 14th–34th Street

Westside 14th–34th Street

Queens

Staten Island

Index by Points of Interest

Actor's Playhouse

Altman's

American Museum of Natural History

American Museum of the Moving Image

American Stock Exchange

Apollo Theater

Beacon Theater

Biograph Cinema

Bowery

Bloomingdale's

Broadway Theaters
South of 48th St.

North of 48th St.

Grand Central Terminal

Guggenheim Museum

Holland Tunnel

Joyce Theater

Lincoln Center

Lincoln Tunnel

Lord & Taylor

Lutece

Macy's Herald Square

Index by Nationality or Specialty

Greek

Ice Cream

Indian

Irish-American

Italian

Italian-Cajun

Japanese

Jewish

Korean

Mexican

Middle Eastern

Peruvian

Pizza

Polish

Russian

Seafood

Soul

Thai

Index by Classification

Ethnic Treasure

Funky Casual

A Little Romance

Positively NYC

Wholesome Hideaway